In Pursuit

CONFESSIONS OF A GAY CATHOLIC TEENAGER

BY ALEX JAMES SANTIAGO

LIFE TEEN

Authored by Alex James Santiago.

Designed by Casey Olson.

Copy editing by Christina Mead and Joel Stepanek.

ISBN: 978-0-9962385-2-6

Published by Life Teen, Inc.
2222 S. Dobson Rd.
Suite 601
Mesa, AZ 85202

LifeTeen.com
Printed in the United States of America.
Printed on acid-free paper.

For more information about Life Teen or to order additional copies, go online to LifeTeen.com or call us at 1-800-809-3902.

EDITOR'S NOTE

Although the terms "gay" and "lesbian" are used freely in popular culture, the Catholic Church encourages us to use the phrase "person who experiences same-sex attractions" in order to acknowledge the dignity of the human person, whose identity isn't found in their sexual orientation but rather in their Creator (CCC 2357-2358). We, at Life Teen, wholeheartedly accept this distinction and emphatically agree with the Church that our humanity is not to be solely defined by one's sexuality, attractions, or desires.

With this in mind, you will notice that in the first part of the book, the word "gay" is used frequently by the author as he tells his story. We chose not to edit this out because it is reflective of his personal journey and understanding of the terminology as it relates to who he is first and foremost as a son of God. As his conversion progresses and his relationship with God deepens, you will notice a change in the language he uses to describe himself in Chapter 8 and continuing throughout the rest of the book. We hope that this purposeful use of language can be seen as a tool to engage the culture where it's at and aid in walking the reader slowly into the depth of truth that God offers to us about our sexuality.

Special thanks to all of our content editors who helped with the creation of this book: Mark Hart, Fr. Dan Felton, Fr. Robert Schreiner, Fr. Dan Beeman, Fr. Michael Silloway, Tina Nair, Hudson Byblow, Eve Tushnet, and Melinda Selmys

TABLE OF CONTENTS

INTRODUCTION

My words cannot express how beautifully nerve-wracking it is for me to write about the deepest depths of my soul, and about the amount of intense love that God has for us. It can be a bit difficult to be vulnerable with each other... but hey, that's what we learn from Jesus' crucifixion right? Complete surrender of yourself for the sake of others, all motivated by self-sacrificial love. That's exactly why I said, "yes," to writing this book; it's a response to a call of the Lord. I really have felt God place this uncontainable love in my heart for you as a reader, and that's why I'm sharing my life with you. It is necessary to know how God can reach into the messiest and darkest parts of our lives, and that's why this book is for YOU. Maybe you feel like you're at the summit of your Catholic faith, or maybe you're barely grasping onto any hope that God exists. You are all my brothers and sisters, and I have you all in my prayers. Whether you identify as straight, gay, lesbian, bisexual, or transgender – I'm looking out for you! And so is the Lord. He loves you. Jesus carries this radiant joy, a glory that is far beyond our ability to comprehend. I've engaged in a deeper relationship with this person, the person of Jesus Christ, and it has radically changed my life.

I don't have all the answers on how to live the best possible life as a Catholic teen who experiences same-sex attraction. In high school, I was largely in denial, played football and ran track, and nobody suspected that I even struggled with this. Now I'm 19, a freshman in college, and still trying to figure out this whole thing myself. I've honestly gone to bed at night thinking, "*God, so what's going to happen to me? Like seriously 'cause I have no clue...*" And while God hasn't given me all the answers, He's given me hope, forgiveness, tender mercy, and sensitive love. God has filled so many deep voids and longings in my heart that no person, drug, lustful pleasure, or earthly thing could possibly satisfy. Had I never allowed God's hope into my heart, I don't know if I would have even lived life to the fullest during high school. God has been there to love me through my sweetest victories and my worst defeats.

Now, I've managed to work up enough trust (the thing I sometimes lack the most) to simply hand over my same-sex attractions to Him. I've decided to find complete comfort and solace in Him alone and let go of the chains of fear that held me down for so long. God has this nice way of making beautiful things out of the stuff in our lives that give us the most trouble. The lyrics to "*Nothing I Hold On To*" by Will Reagan pretty much speak to my soul when it comes to giving it all away:

"I lean not on my own understanding
My life is in the hands of the Maker of heaven
I give it all to You God
trusting that You'll make something beautiful out of me
I will climb this mountain with my hands wide open
There's nothing I hold on to."

I hope this book will do two things: First, I hope that it will be a good insight for anybody who wants to know what it's like to experience same-sex attractions. Second, I hope it shows you how Jesus has ultimately given me new life. The struggle of being gay is very real and very heavy at times. But I'm still just a normal teenager, and this is my story. This is the guy I've always been – inside and out.

1

ARE YOU GAY?

"Are you gay?"

The first time my dad asked me that question I was only 7 years old. It was the hardest day of my childhood. My dad sat me down in the bathroom one afternoon (mom couldn't hear us there) so that we could have a talk. He began to go on and on about how one of his friends from work had a son who recently came out as gay. My dad said that I needed to shape up and stop acting so gay. It wasn't right for me to be so flamboyant.

He then looked me in the eyes and asked, "Are you gay?" I remember looking down at the floor as I began to cry. I didn't even understand the question but all I knew was that I didn't want to be "gay" because according to my dad it was a *terrible* thing, something that no dad wanted his son to be. With tears running down my face I choked out the words, "No Daddy, why would you ask me that?"

Yeah, it was a rough day.

I knew my parents cared about me. In fact, before I was born the doctor told them that it would be better to abort me. In the beginning months of my mother's pregnancy her appendix burst, and according to the doctors I was not supposed to make it out of her womb alive. If I did, they said I would be highly deformed. My mom was devastated beyond belief, and she and my dad weren't sure how to handle the situation. They spent many nights praying and asking for Our Lady's intercession. They did not want to lose me, no matter the cost; they wanted to fight for me, and so they chose life.

I'm so grateful to my parents for that. And I can honestly say that my parents did their absolute best to make sure I had the childhood that every kid dreamed of. I knew my dad loved me, but I only genuinely felt that love before I turned 5 years old, *before* I became "flamboyant" in his eyes.

Recently, my mom and I were watching old home videos of me as a kid. As we watched the videos, I saw my dad pick me up, kiss me on the cheek, and then set me down on the kitchen counter to talk with me. I was his pal, and I knew that he loved me then. As I leaned my head on my mom's arm while we were watching the video, I couldn't help but wonder, *"Why did this stop the moment my dad began to think I was gay?"*

I used to be such a vibrant, bright, and talkative kid. I loved life and all the people around me. For a brief time, I was happy and content. But then my dad started to have talks with me about how I needed to man up and be more "masculine." He said that if I didn't change people were going to think I was gay, and worse yet I would be made fun of when I got older. He said that it would be hard for me to make friends if I didn't change. When he told me that I felt like a confused puppy looking into his angry owner's eyes thinking, *"What? I don't understand what's wrong with me?"* As a 7-year-old boy, I barely even knew what the words gay, faggot, and flamboyant meant, but I heard them all.

I didn't know what to think about myself. I began to hang out with lots of girls because I really didn't feel masculine... or at least I wasn't a "man" according to my dad's definition of a man. I distanced myself from boys because they were something that felt foreign to me. I don't know why I was so nervous to be around them. I think I was afraid that they were going to make fun of me the way my dad said they would. My insecurity was off the charts; I couldn't do anything considered "masculine" in the right way.

I couldn't even participate in sports with confidence. When I was in the 3rd grade, I thought I played sports wrong because I could possibly be "gay," as my dad phrased it. I was so unsure of myself and my abilities that I felt I was no longer good enough to be a boy.

Now I know that being a "man" isn't defined by how good we are at sports but rather the way we hold God in our hearts, but at that time I really felt I must have done all the guy things wrong because my dad thought I was "gay."

I was the nerd of my class, and that meant that I was treated differently than everybody else. Being left out and being pushed around did not help whatsoever in my ability to feel masculine. My self-image was torn to pieces by every joke made about me and having no guy friends just added to the problem. I began to make friends exclusively with the girls in my class because they didn't make fun of me. I wanted guy friends, but being accepted by girls helped me feel secure and not judged. Friendship was something that seemed foreign to me. The few times I actually managed to have a guy friend over, I was terribly nervous and gave off the impression that I wasn't comfortable in my own skin. All I wanted was to not be judged. I felt that the way I was – who I was – just wasn't okay with everybody. I felt very abandoned. I felt like everything about me was just *wrong*.

My comfort zone became my mother's arms and the kind gentleness of other girls. The more foreign males became to me, the more I longed for love and acceptance from them.

Pretty soon my dad noticed I was not "improving" in his eyes, and he decided to implement a whole new plan to make me more masculine. When I was in elementary school, my dad bought me workout equipment that would specifically make me move my hands and arms differently so that my gestures would become less feminine. Talk about crushing the last bit of self-confidence I had. I knew my dad was only trying to help me, and he was doing this out of love, but at the same time it only made me feel so much worse. All I longed for was to be loved unconditionally by him like when I was a toddler. I wanted to be hugged by him without me feeling like he was ashamed of who I was and the way I was perceived by other people.

I was constantly being told by him to "stop moving my arms and hands like a girl" and to "talk deeper"; it made the thought of me possibly being gay consume my mind. At this point in my life, whenever I was approached by boys, girls, teachers, uncles, aunts, or cousins, my first thought was, "*Do they think I'm gay? I really hope they don't think I'm gay. If I give off the impression that I'm gay, they won't be my friend or they'll treat me differently and totally stop being nice to me. They'll judge me or won't love me or will stop treating me like a normal person.*" I would be asked by other boys, "Hey dude? Are you gay? Ha, you're such a queer, I swear." It literally felt like I had this huge spotlight on me every time I was so rudely questioned like that. I felt like a piece of dirt when guys would ask me this; especially if they mentioned that they "heard" from other people that I was gay.

Even when I thought I was making friends, I couldn't escape bullying. I performed in a talent show with a group of guys, and as we waited our turn, they were talking about how nervous they were for the show. One guy named Anthony said, "Since we're all wearing pink button-ups and dancing to a song from the movie *Grease*, why don't we pop our collars?" We were all performing together, so I popped my collar along with them and got ready to line up backstage with the rest of our group. It was almost our turn. Then Anthony looked at me and said, "I wasn't telling *you* to pop your collar *too,* faggot." The other boys laughed, and my heart sank inside. I was only 10 years old.

Bullying hurts. It's never okay. I experienced bullying because of my sexuality. When a part of you that is so tender and so sacred is made fun of, it is extremely detrimental to your development as a whole, regardless of whether you experience same-sex attractions or not. For me, it just added to the confusion of who I am as a human being. I was making every effort to be accepted, and I consistently felt like a failure. I felt like I was literally born a screw-up.

2

GYM CLASS

Looking back, it's kind of funny how much I was in denial of being gay – especially since I felt like my biggest task in middle school was "Overcoming P.E."

Let me just explain what it's like being in denial, and how difficult it was for me to experience these attractions. At school, I dreaded the days we had P.E. (physical education). Every time I would go into the locker room to change, I found myself trying not to stare at the other 6th, 7th, and 8th graders changing. I would ask myself, "*Why was I trying not to stare? Why was it that I could not help but want to look? Why was it that I was insanely attracted to the other older boys changing in the room?*" It was weird because while I would talk with the guys during P.E. our conversations were based on how "hot" the 8th grade girls were, and in the back of my mind I was thinking about how "hot" the 8th grade *guys* were that were talking to me! The fact that I was attracted to those guys only made me shy and insecure when talking to them. The same way a guy would probably feel a bit insecure talking to a girl he thought was pretty, or vice versa for a female trying to talk to a cute guy. I was so confused to say the least.

This is where lust really began to creep its way into my life. Picture this: If a 12-year-old boy with heterosexual attractions was inside a locker room full of girls in their underwear, how would that make him feel, or act, or react? Seriously think about it... Yep. Well, that was me... but stuck in a room full of boys. I had no control over what I was feeling and it was not like I could "avoid the near occasion of sin" by not being in P.E. because it's like an educational law to be in P.E... so I was pretty stuck. At the time I was telling myself, "*Stop being attracted to them, don't get sexually enticed when they talk to you about their experimentation with girls, don't allow yourself to want to see them change or look at them while changing.*" I felt so divided within myself, and I really did not know what to do.

To add to all of this, I also wanted to make more friends, and I wanted to be popular. At my middle school, being in football would help you gain a lot of "cool points"... so I was totally up for joining it. I also thought that I would make my dad proud of me because that meant I was going to be more masculine, which is what he wanted.

The day tryouts came around I was nervous the whole day. My stomach felt like it was stirred up on the inside, and I had no confidence in myself whatsoever. When I walked out onto the field, I remember thinking, "*I am going to do this. I am not going to be the wimp I once was. Enough is enough.*" I then prayed the only small prayer I could ring up out of me.

"*Jesus, help me to do good as I try out. I want to do well. Amen.*" I wasn't exactly confident in my own prayers either.

"Hey, good job kid! You just can't be afraid to get hit okay?" the coached yelled at me.

"Alright coach," I replied, still not too confident in myself or what I was doing. I was trying out for running back because my dad was a fan of the Dallas Cowboys, and he loved their running back at the time. I really felt that if I could play this sport well enough, he wouldn't think I was gay or flamboyant. I thought maybe, just maybe, he would make me feel good about myself again.

Unfortunately, my insecurities got the best of me. I quit football after a couple weeks just before we got to the hitting stages of practice. One of the coaches knew my mom and told her, "I don't know why your son quit. He was actually pretty good. He just can't be afraid of hitting or getting."

To simply hear my coach say that I was good at what I was doing, it made me feel like a man for the first time in my life. It felt good to be praised for something I did right, despite the fact that I felt like I was not an ideal representation of a pre-teen boy. Praise was something I felt I really lacked the most from my dad. It was the lack of praise that made me feel small and far from confident in who I was. Because I was previously "too girly," my father held back from any praise he could give me and just focused so much on making me a completely straight, tough guy. I never got any positive attention from him.

Simply hearing an older man praise me in the smallest way possible lit up my whole world. I finally did something right. I actually felt loved. I realized that there were just certain insecurities I needed to overcome, certain feelings and emotions that I could not let control the way I responded to life. I remember thanking God for some sort of masculinity, or at least for making me feel like a regular boy for once in the world's terms. I ended up doing cross-country, basketball, track, and baseball instead of football. During track season, I felt like I finally gained some guy friends.

I remember the first time I had one of them over to hang out, I had never felt happier in my life. When he came over, his mom called him and asked what he was doing and he said, "Oh I'm hanging out with one of my friends from school, he's a nerd, but he's cool!" I felt so relieved to finally not be treated differently. For once, I was not worried about if I came off as feminine or not. I could just be me, and that was all my heart desired.

However, I still had doubts and insecurities. Since I'd never had guy friends before, I didn't exactly know how to handle their friendship. They still sometimes asked if I was gay because they had heard that rumor. I, of course, told them I was most definitely not gay. I didn't want to be that one guy that would overthink everything and assume things about people, but those questions led me to feel like those guys weren't *really* friends with me. I came up with crazy ideas about how it must have been impossible for them to be friends with me – a guy who was accused of being gay.

I was left longing for something that would put an end to my insecurities, and crush the feminine perceptions of me that others had: something that would make me feel wholly alive, content, and happy. Little did I know the answer was going to come in an encounter with God.

3

HE MADE MOM CRY

As a young teenager, I had a stirring in my heart for something. I didn't know what it was, but it was very real. That feeling was a desire for Christ, and as I grew closer to entering high school I was about to learn about Him through my mom. My family became involved with a Catholic Retreat Movement called A.C.T.S. Seeing my parents both go on this retreat completely changed the dynamics of my family forever.

One afternoon, after my mom had been on retreat, I got home from school and was not sure what to think of what I saw. My mom was upstairs looking at a painting of the crucifixion, weeping bitterly.

I didn't understand why she was crying. It didn't click for me how the cross ultimately means we are free from the chains of our past. The cross means that we are free from the circumstances we do not choose to be in... whether that means you are fatherless, or bullied, or feel like you don't have it all together, or, in my case, experience same-sex attractions. We can be free from the scars of harsh words and cruel punishments if we choose to surrender the deepest and most secret parts of our sensitive hearts to Him.

Seeing my mother cry was the first time I realized that this whole "God thing" was something that transcends far past the walls of a small Catholic Church. It was the first time I tangibly saw that Jesus actually *cares* about people and that His Spirit moves in people's hearts and fills their souls.

When my mom came downstairs, I asked her why she was crying. And she told me, "I don't know... on that retreat, after I received Communion I remembered the words of Christ, 'Take this, all of you, and drink from it, for this is the chalice of my blood, the blood of the new and eternal covenant, which will be poured out for you and for many, for the forgiveness of sins. Do this in memory of Me.' And the choir started singing a song that kept repeating, 'what can wash away my sins, what can make me whole again? Nothing but the blood, nothing but the blood of Jesus,' and I just could not control my crying. And then the song said, 'what can make us white as snow, nothing but the blood of Jesus,' and I could not hold back anymore. It felt amazing and I felt like the hurt of my childhood was finally healed."

I had no clue how to respond to my mom after that. Although I was only 12, what she said seemed to make perfect sense. I felt lost for words but found in my thoughts. I wondered what that felt like. What is it like to feel God? What is it like to know Him? What is it like to be healed? Having been raised in a moderately good and financially stable family, unlike my mom, I had no clue what being burdened felt like for her, or how liberation felt.

I continued to see God working in the lives of my family after the retreat. Even my uncle who once lived a life consumed by earthly things did a complete 180-degree turn with his life after encountering God on retreat. He no longer was okay with living a semi-virtuous life. He told my dad he regretted ever comparing himself to other people based off the amount of money they made, and he regretted ever allowing his son to go to strip clubs and have dirty hotel parties. He realized that a life filled with things of the world only lasts for a short season and that a life filled with things from the Eternal God above lasts forever.

I was 12 years old at this time, and seeing my dad and uncle talk about all these things made my heart long for something similar. I felt like God's hand was gently tugging at my heart, and I wanted to allow myself to feel more of Him. My dad told me there was also a teen's retreat; I couldn't wait to go!

So this is the part where I go on the retreat and have an amazing experience right? Actually no, my dad felt that I should wait until

I was in high school to go on the retreat. "I don't want to wait," I thought, "I want to experience God NOW."

Instead, my dad signed me up for a small retreat at our city's diocesan headquarters. The retreat flew by for me, but I did not exactly feel any different. Little did I know that sometimes Christ's presence overcomes us like the way the sun warms our body. If you picture yourself sitting outside on the beach, allowing the rays to touch your skin, at first it's slightly noticeable but as time progresses, the heat builds up and up, and then the warmth increases to a point that our skin is overwhelmed by it. That's how God works sometimes.

After the diocesan retreat had ended, my dad told me that we would be going to a community function that involved a portion of the Teen A.C.T.S. retreat.

I walked into the conference room where the teens on retreat would come in, and I sat down in the back with my dad. The room was hot because of the summer weather and damp because of a light rain that fell over the city earlier that day. When the teens arrived, they began to sing their retreat theme song. All the members of the community that were present stood up and began to sing the song along with them. I stood up too and began singing. As the chorus of the song repeated over and over again, my voice began to crack, I felt my heart wrench, and warm tears began to roll down my cheeks. "*I will walk by faith, even when I cannot see. Well, because this broken road, prepares your will for me.*" I kept singing those words with all I had inside of me and just let what felt like God's overwhelming waters cleanse my soul. I bitterly wept, and I did not know why. I just knew that what was coming into the deep recesses of my soul was God. I felt Him. I couldn't stop crying. And then for whatever reason, after the song ended I just kept crying uncontrollably. So many of the adults from my parish community came up to me and embraced me. After a couple of minutes passed, my weeping turned into small gasps for air, and then faded into a peaceful breath.

Every night that summer, I went to bed smiling. I really did. I knew what it was like to feel uplifted by God. Although I cried and had my first encounter with Him, I had no idea that the whole experience was just Jesus saying, "Son, you think I'm going to be finished with you anytime soon? Nope! We are just getting started..."

The song that hit me is called *Walk by Faith* by Jeremy Camp. I think my iPod kept count of about 200 replays of that song. I was obsessed with it. At night, before I fell asleep, I would leave the window open to let the cool, summer breeze fill my room, and I would play that song out loud, recounting that first moment I had with God over and over again; that moment when I was drowned in the beautiful undertow of the presence of Jesus. I felt so happy that I had the opportunity to feel Him and begin to know Him. The gravity of what people thought about me seemed to fade behind the glory of God's goodness. It was out-weighed. My self-esteem rose substantially, and it was because I was finding my self-worth in Him rather than in my peers.

4

CUE CONFUSION

I felt content with who I was, just a young boy who loved God. That was all that really mattered to me. I had a renewed sense of confidence because of Jesus Christ, and I felt like I could now befriend pretty much anybody.

For the first time ever, I felt like I could be myself and not feel like I was being judged for being too "feminine." It just blew my mind because I knew that I was still the same person I had always been on the inside, but just because I was more "manly" I was finally accepted by all the guys as opposed to being treated harshly and deprived of the dignity a human being deserves.

I wasn't really bothered by that realization at first, but I felt so dejected at the fact that I missed so many opportunities to meet and have deep friendship, to have intimate brotherhood, all because beforehand I came off as a "faggot" or a "queer."

I had always wanted to be friends with the popular kids, and now it was finally happening. I ran cross-country, played basketball, ran track, and was a team manager for baseball. When all the popular guys finally acknowledged my existence and talked to me, I didn't know whether to feel blessed or angry. Why was it that only a couple years before, I was the odd one out because of old rumors that led people to question my sexuality? I hated it.

Besides that resentment, it was also difficult to be friends with guys that were popular because the majority of them were good looking. I felt conflicted because they were cute in my eyes; they were in shape, and I would find myself thinking about them at home all the time or when I went to bed. I was attracted to them. They didn't realize I was low-key crushing on them, and when they would talk to me about girls. I would do my best to play along, but I could hardly relate. Of course, at this point in my life, I still did not consider myself gay. I just simply thought, "*I don't know why I'm getting sexually attracted to these guys when I'm with them... but I need to stop.*" Shortly after this, I experienced two new realities that would only magnify this confusion: dating girls and watching gay porn.

I tried to date girls. I wanted to fit in with the guys, and it seemed like everyone was dating. I also felt that dating girls would help me feel better about myself, and would especially help the guys stop questioning if I was gay. Even though I was more attracted to guys, I wasn't blind to beauty in women. I told the guys about different crushes I had on girls who I thought were cute. I played the game so well to make it seem like I was crushing on them that I made myself believe it. I found myself catching some feelings for them, but I just couldn't feel a deep connection or attraction. I didn't get how the rest of the guys were so "in love" with their girlfriends.

I even tried to tell a girl I liked her. It was awkward, and I was rejected. Yeah, although I was more attracted to guys it definitely sucked to be rejected.

Around this time, I made a best friend named Emma. This girl was genuinely gorgeous, and a lot of the guys from my school hit on her, and they began to question if we had a thing for each other. She would simply tell them, "No, he's like my brother, guys." She told me everything, as I did with her. Throughout our growing friendship, she vented to me about her various boyfriend problems and her first sexual experiences with them, and I would tell her how I never really kissed a girl or had a girlfriend. Wanting to be a good friend, I would tell her she should try to avoid doing those things simply because God didn't want her to do them. I loved how we could be so brutally honest with each other.

At times, my emotions led me to be deeply attracted to her, but I didn't know if I was attracted to her in a heterosexual way, or simply in just a deep, pure, human way. The closer we got, the more I told her about my pursuit for God's heart – the whole furious love affair. It was compelling to see what just sharing my faith with someone did. She was born and raised Catholic, and she became curious about the reality of who God really is. My love for that girl grew so deep and so personal. The closer I got to her, the more we talked about what we were looking for in a prospective boyfriend/ girlfriend. All I said was that I wanted my girlfriend to love God.

One day at school, she asked me when I was expecting to have my first kiss. "I don't know," I said. "I just want to make sure it's with somebody I really like and not a random hookup." She then said, "I mean if you ever want your first kiss you can just tell me..." My heart then began to beat really fast. *"I want to kiss her!"* I thought. *"Or do I?"* It was as if the desire to kiss her wasn't something that came to me naturally. It was something forced because that's how I knew I was *supposed to feel* toward a girl.

"Emma, I mean, I don't know... you're my best friend, and I wouldn't want your boyfriend to get mad..." We left it at that. It really was confusing for me. I felt so lost trying to figure out my own emotions and gauge what I was really feeling.

Along with this growing importance of one's relationship status at the oh-so-young age of 13, lust became a greater struggle. When I was 13, I was exposed to pornography for the first time. One of my friends showed me some porn in the locker room during P.E., and as he stared obviously at the female, I stared at the male. I couldn't help it. I was nervous because I didn't want him to notice I was attracted to the guy rather than the girl. After that first experience of porn, I found myself starting to watch straight porn, but I kept looking at the guy. At first, it was out of curiosity, and I didn't know why I wanted to see the male human body exposed. I craved it... and I would try lusting over the females, but I couldn't lust as easily and naturally as I did over the males.

It didn't help that so many of the conversations I had with my guy friends were about what they did sexually with girls and "how far they'd gone." When they asked me what I'd done with a girl, and when I wanted to have sex, I would respond that I didn't want to do anything to disrespect a woman. I wanted to wait until marriage because I loved God, and I knew it was the right thing to do. I would say this even though I knew I was immensely attracted to guys. Either way, I could hear my dad's voice in the back of my head always telling me to respect girls, and that I should never cross boundaries that would lead me to sin. I wish my dad would have told me to just respect both genders overall because I didn't feel like I was sinning when I was lusting over the guys in front of me. It didn't dawn on me that I was doing the wrong thing.

The more the guys began to fall into these sins of impurity, the more they would open up and share with me. I would give them the best advice I could on drawing close to Jesus and asking Him to give them strength to turn away. They'd ask me how it was so easy for me to not do any of those things with girls, and I would simply say, "I don't know, I just don't want to do it."

I wished I could see my brothers in Christ as just brothers, but it was so difficult. Guys being guys, they were always fooling around in the locker room, flashing each other and just being stupid. As my addiction to porn, especially gay porn, worsened, the more I wished for them to fool around and flash each other so I could be sexually satisfied. It was wrong.

Despite this cycle of sin and confusion, I found myself really happy with the clique of friends I made. They were honestly good people, in spite of their struggles and addictions to drugs, porn, or sex – similar to my own broken self. It felt good to be loved and cared for by them. It felt good to be thought of as a normal human for once and to be accepted. All I knew was that no matter what orientation people were, no matter if they were a jock, skater, emo, prep, etc., we all wanted to be accepted by other people and be loved. This is what we were made for; *we were made for love.* Makes sense... because we're made by a God who is love.

Even though I knew I was sinful (as we all are), I still was madly in love with Jesus, and I didn't want that to change. I knew that deep down all I wanted was to bring other teens to God. I wanted to tell them how He made me feel. My soul was on fire for Him, and I wanted to know more. I wanted to grow closer to God, and I wanted Him to make me into a better son. But I was still in denial that lusting after other guys was a sin, and I never prayed for the conversion of my own heart... at least not yet.

5

FRESHMAN

"Alright... eight, nine, ten. Next set!!" Coach Garcia blew the whistle. The doors at the end of the football weight room were wide open to let in the warm summer breeze. It smelled like metal, sweat, and gross gym clothes. I was with four friends lifting weights. That summer going into my freshman year of high school, I decided to join football, and this time stick to it for the whole year. Being around all the guys during the summer months meant that we were all trying to establish ourselves and trying to carry any impressive part of our middle school reputation into the new social groups we were making. The beginning stages of high school always seem so crucial. It seems as if the gravity of who we are lies in making ourselves known based on the clothes we wear, the way we talk, and the way we handle our friendships. Fortunately, I didn't seem to worry as much about if people thought I was gay.

After a few weeks, a couple of guys and I finally developed into our own solid social group. Again, I found it difficult to not stare at the guys but I was discreet about it and they never even noticed. I didn't know if I just admired their bodies and wanted to get into better physical shape myself, or if I was just extremely attracted to them.

I was still in denial. It seemed like being attracted to them was something I needed to fight off. I would sometimes wonder if they felt the same way. I mean like I said before, growing up, guys tended to flash each other a lot. I didn't know if it was because they were just being silly, if they were kind of attracted to guys themselves, or if they just wanted to show off. I knew that when I would flash them they would look too, so I just had no clue what the truth was anymore.

Along with joining football, I had the opportunity to experience something else quite memorable that summer. I signed up for a Teen A.C.T.S. retreat. There were things I heard, experienced, and witnessed from other teens that left me feeling so fortunate to have the family and life that I had. The friendships I made there became so deep because the spirit of Christ welded them together. I had never realized what it meant to hold others close to my heart and close to God at the same time. The love I had for those brothers and sisters in Christ felt like a deep prayer itself.

However, going into high school seemed to dehydrate those friendships, and make my relationship with God dry up to almost nothing. I very quickly got caught up in being what I thought was a better and more popular version of me. I changed up my wardrobe to look like the cooler upperclassmen guys. I really began to worry extensively about my self-image, about having the most followers on Twitter and Instagram, about how many people knew who I was, and about befriending all the pretty girls because that's what it meant to be a "guy" in high school; one with game and one with lots of friends. Popularity became my god. Pretty soon I was doing all the things I had vowed I'd never do.

One Friday afternoon I felt an itch to do something rebellious. My friends and I planned to go over to my friend's house because his parents would let us binge drink without any limitations. His garage was filled with people from school. There was loud music, and the smell of smoke and alcohol filled the air. I ended up drinking beer and a couple of other drinks I couldn't even identify. Since I was a dumb freshman, at the end of the night, I called my dad for a ride and thought he wouldn't notice the strong smell of alcohol radiating from me. When he picked me up, he also drove a couple of my friends to their homes. And of course, my dad quickly noticed they were acting strange. To top it off, my friend Gabriel threw up in my car. When I got home, my dad asked me if I drank anything. I told him, "No." Then he said, "AJ, you think I'm stupid? I can smell the alcohol, and your friends were drunk. I would rather you admit to me the truth than lie to my face. I don't know if I can trust you now."

I never felt so disgusted with myself before. It was my first time being busted for anything seriously bad by my parents, and I knew that letting them down made me feel like a complete mess-up. My parents worked hard and put a roof over my head, and I violated the trust of the people I should be respecting most. I couldn't sleep that night.

A couple weeks later, there was a party happening that I wanted to go to only because a guy who trash-talked about my sister was going to be there. I wanted to show my face and see what happened.

"Dad, can I please go to this party?"

He said, "No, why would you want to go to a place when somebody you don't like will be there and where there is going to be underage drinking? And to top it off, you haven't been acting quite well either. You've disrespected your mom, me, and your sister. Enough is enough. I don't know what gave you decency to even ask. Sit down."

As soon as he said that I got up, kicked the living room table and ran for the car keys. "You better not think you're going to take the car over there either. Get back in here!" Dad shouted. I continued out the door and into my family's truck. As I sat there, I felt sick to my stomach knowing that I was in BIG trouble. I had received big punishments before because of my attitude since I had started high school, and I felt like this was probably the last straw for me. I really felt my dad was going to do something terrible to me.

After some contemplation, I got out of the truck and went back inside. I quickly ran upstairs to my room, closed the door, and turned on the lights. Then, my dad barged in. He yelled, "Give me your phone NOW!" Bewildered, I handed it to him. We started shouting at each other, and he threw my phone against the wall. It shattered to pieces. I'd never felt so much anger toward my dad. When he left the room, I laid down on the bed and started crying out of anger, frustration, and guilt. I didn't know what to think of myself.

My dad's voice woke me up the next morning. "Get up." It was 5:00 a.m. "We're going to have a long talk."

My dad made me get dressed and get into our truck. We took off down the freeway. We drove to a nearby city, about two hours away. It was the most awkward car ride ever; we didn't say a word the whole way. It was around Christmas time, so it was chilly outside, and snow was gently falling. I began to think...

"What in the world has been up with me? I have a terrible attitude. I used to be the kid who talked about God to my friends, who used to be humble and kind-hearted, who used to be so appreciative of all my family did for me. Now I am some stuck-up brat who puts down others because they seem like losers to me."

I was using terms like "faggot," "queer," and "loser" when I spoke about other people. I had fallen into so many serious sins at this point, and my addiction to pornography had gotten worse. I went from watching porn a few times a week, to watching porn and masturbating multiple times a day. I continued to have lustful thoughts over my guy friends, and I knew this was disrespectful of their human dignity. I felt like I couldn't escape so many sins because I was so attached to fulfilling my own distorted desires.

And where was my relationship with God? The One who brought me so much peace, who gave me confidence, who filled my heart with an uncontainable love? He was nowhere to be found in my life at that point. My faith life had dwindled down to nothing, almost to a point that I barely had any belief in the existence of God. I became so consumed with things of the world that I didn't want to associate myself with church anymore. I just wanted to do whatever it took to be popular and fulfill my sexual cravings.

After a two-hour drive of deep contemplation, we arrived at a forest amidst a cloudy sky, frosty air, and a light snowfall. My dad then told me to help him cut down a Christmas tree for our house. We took turns taking a whack at the tree. He then asked me, "So what's been up with you? Why have you been so angry? You're not yourself anymore. And mom and I have noticed that." I snapped back fueled by the disgust I felt for myself, "I don't know, Dad!" We continued cutting the tree and eventually loaded it up onto the truck and took off home. We talked a little more on the way back, but I was embarrassed to admit why I had been acting so poorly.

That whole experience was a reality check. Why was I acting so rebellious if I already knew who God was and is?

Toward the end of my freshman year, my parish finally started its own youth group, and the youth minister asked me to help with a Confirmation retreat. She gathered up a whole bunch of teens who had previously been to Teen A.C.T.S. We served over 400 teens on the retreat, and the size of the youth group rose to about 50 kids. After messing up so much, I never thought that God would want to use to me again. God used my own life to help other teens who had no previous tangible experience with Him, even though I myself was broken. The fact that Jesus did that gave me hope. It made me realize that my God was still pursuing me, even if I wasn't pursuing Him.

A few weeks after that, I restlessly got ready for bed. It was late, so late my parents and sister were long asleep. I remember thinking, *"I want to know what a second redemption feels like after knowing God. I used to be that one good kid who got good grades and had good morals and everything, and now I just feel like a hypocrite serving God while acting like I don't know Him."* As I sat down on my bed, I decided to play the Christian music station on my phone. I began to enter into a deep reflection on my life and how I had come to know God. Then on the radio a couple of piano notes started to play. You know some sort of deep emotional song is about to go down when high piano notes start off the melody... The lyrics to the song said:

"But you love me anyway...
See now, I am the man who yelled out from the crowd
For Your blood to be spilled on this earth shaking ground
Yes then I turned away with the smile on my face
With this sin in my heart tried to bury Your grace
And then alone in the night I still called out for You
So ashamed of my life, my life, my life

But You love me anyway
Oh, God, how you love me
Yes, You love me anyway
It's like nothing in life that I've ever known
Yes, You love me anyway
Oh, Lord, how You love me."

(*You Love Me Anyway*, by Sidewalk Prophets)

I felt the hot tears begin to force their way out of my eyes and roll down my cheeks. My heart wrenched inside of me, and I grunted trying to not have a breakdown. As the song continued, I just couldn't hold it back. I fell back on my bed, covered my face with my arms and started crying.

"I'm so sorry God. I am so, so sorry," was my prayer that night.

As the days passed, I got a phone call and was asked to help on another retreat. I knew that I had just barely made up with God and was just barely starting to change for the better, but I still wanted to help. I said, "Yes." Formation for the retreat weekend took 13 weeks, and the team grew very close during all that time. The connection and love I had for my friends on the team felt so deeply rooted in my heart.

On the retreat team, there was a guy I instantly became friends with. His name was Greg. He was a 17-year-old junior at the same high school. He was in wrestling. We hung out a lot while at church, and it felt good to have somebody genuinely care for me as much as he did.

Let me just explain what real, pure brotherhood felt like for me, and how crucial it was for my life, especially for a guy who was in denial of being gay. Since my father's love seemed to be stripped away when I was little, there was a part of me that longed for an older male's affection. I just wanted to be loved. I didn't want lust or anything. *I just wanted love*. There were places in my life where I just wanted a man, in particular, to care for me as a son or brother. I don't think I longed for that because I had an attraction to men... I just knew it was something I needed. This friend, more like an older brother of mine, filled that gap in my heart without even realizing it. The thing he did that impacted me the most was when I had to give a personal testimony on the retreat, and he introduced me before I walked into the room. He said, "I've only known this guy for a couple weeks, but I've gotten really close to him. I really look at him as a younger brother that I've always wished to have, and I love him a lot."

It's hard for me into put to words how that made me feel... I just know that my heart was filled with love. I was special to the guy I looked up to as a role model. I think this made me feel so good because I hardly felt special to my dad.

As a guy who had been previously accused of being gay in my younger years, it felt so good to openly receive this love from Greg. He loved me for me and actually never questioned if I was attracted to guys. I knew I wasn't coming off as gay anymore, and I never told Greg later on that I realized I was attracted to men, but at that time in my life, I received what I felt was a great gift from

God – the treasure of Catholic brotherhood. This totally changed my outlook on the way it felt to look at porn. Greg was a handsome guy, but God used him and a few other older male role models to begin a change in the lustful desires of my heart.

6

#THESTRUGGLEISREAL

After helping on that retreat, I made a decision to follow Christ, but this time I was far more serious about my commitment. It was time to stop being so mediocre in where I stood with Jesus in my faith. I wanted to stop being swayed so easily by my peers, my friends, and by what society said was worth living for. It was time for me to stop making popularity such a huge priority in my life. There is absolutely nothing wrong with having lots of friends; it was just time for me to live and be myself without caring so much about what other people thought.

It was a bold decision to follow Christ, and lots of my friends were not too thrilled about it. As the weeks passed; they all started to trickle away. I also made the decision to not do sports and as a result I lost a huge amount of the social connection I had with my high school class. To make matters worse, I severely broke out with acne... like I literally had loads of it on my face. My confidence level hit an all-time low, worse than what I had experienced before.

Every day I ate lunch by myself. That hurt a lot. Being self-conscious about my now pimple-infested face caused me to feel like I was not attractive anymore or even socially acceptable to anybody, period. I'll never forget when a little girl pointed at me and said, “Daddy, why does he have mountains on his face?” The father awkwardly pulled his daughter to the side and apologized to me.

Amidst what felt like the end of the world to any high school teenager, I somehow managed to draw closer to Christ. It was through this social isolation that I really found myself pursuing His heart. Whenever I would go to the gym, I would listen to Christian music as I was running. Those were moments of joy and fulfillment. When I would lift weights, I'd let out all the frustration that I had toward every person that I felt screwed me over as a friend. It was the healthiest way I could deal with what I was going through. I was not going to let the world knock me down. My joy was not going to be shaken or taken away! Sorry Satan, NOT TODAY BOY. #PeaceOut

The fall of my freshman year, I went to a quinceañera (a cultural birthday celebration for a 15-year-old Hispanic girl) and met a beautiful girl named Olivia... I decided to like her. As time progressed, I asked her to be my girlfriend. Although I was dating her, I still couldn't develop a deep attachment to her. I knew I liked her... so why didn't I feel anything? Keep in mind I had talked to, or dated, a few girls before but it all felt the same. It didn't feel special. I found myself texting my girlfriend at night and at the same time I would fall into the sin of lust and watch gay porn. I would feel so guilty because first of all, watching porn and masturbating is a sin and second of all, because I felt I was betraying a commitment to my girlfriend by doing it behind her back.

I was frustrated with myself and didn't know why I couldn't break the chains of porn. So, I tried to make myself sexually attracted to my girlfriend by watching straight porn and even lesbian porn. I didn't find myself aroused by it and would have to force myself beyond what I really desired in order to "enjoy" it at all. Like I said, overall watching it was bad, but I felt even worse because I knew I was trying to start a lustful attraction toward women, which ultimately in and of itself isn't right because it's disrespectful and degrading of a girl's dignity. I don't know why it didn't click for me then that watching gay porn was disrespectful of a guy's dignity, too.

I would go over to Olivia's house for lunch, and we had so many opportunities to fall into sexual sin, but the temptation was just never there for me. We didn't even kiss until we were five months into our relationship. It was a quick kiss at a high school football game. I tried to be a good boyfriend and make it as romantic as I possibly could. But I just didn't feel "in love," and I didn't know if it was because I hadn't met the right girl or what. I also didn't know how other guys felt with their girlfriends. I would think, "*Do my guy friends feel just as romantically dry with their girlfriends as I do with mine? Do they feel in love? How do married couples feel? Are they deeply connected and attracted to each other?"* I broke up with Olivia a couple of months later.

You can say I was really confused about my life, or just in deep denial about who I was attracted too. *But all I knew was that my longing for God only increased... dramatically.* I began to spend at least an hour at night praying, because of everything I was feeling – the joy, the confusion, and the longing for a clique of guy friends my own age.

One night I was talking on the phone with a girl from church, and I started to tell her about my life, and how I used to be made fun of because people thought I was gay. She then asked me, "Were you gay before?" I said "What? No, I was not gay before." Keep in mind this is a guy who was struggling with an addiction to gay pornography and was aroused by guys changing in the locker room. The denial was real.

I don't know why it didn't click that I was experiencing same-sex attraction, although I was trying to "fight off" being attracted to guys. I felt confused about whether I was completely homosexual or if it was just because of the lack of male involvement I had as a kid, as well as a variety of other factors.

Around this time, one of my good friends told me about a Catholic youth conference called, "Steubenville." It was a three-day conference that consisted of worship, sacraments, and thousands of teens, basically any Catholic teen's dream.

I told my friend that I wanted to go... and really badly. I signed up at her parish within a few days. I was so stoked. Like beyond belief. I couldn't wait to be there. I was so tired of helping on all these retreats and feeling spiritually dry while all these other teens coming off the retreats felt so close to God. I was so drained from giving all that I could possibly give, and I still had sins I had to get rid of. I knew I improved on treating people as children of God, but I wanted to be wholesome. I had things I needed to let go of. I just knew I needed some sort of healing because I was still holding onto hurt from my childhood and from losing friends my sophomore and junior year. At that point in time, I was stressed because I was tired of not feeling good enough for anybody. I didn't know for certain what I wanted to study in college, and I didn't know why I couldn't maintain a good, authentic love for Christ in my life.

My dad was never pleased with anything I was doing, and if he was pleased, he would never tell me. I was tired of my faith being something that comes and goes, something that just fades with the wind after every retreat. I was tired of going to youth group only for friends and not entering into it to deepen my faith.

I knew I could only do this through God's intervention. I couldn't do it alone.

7

FREEDOM

It took me 17 years to finally admit to someone that I am attracted to men, and it happened in the Sacrament of Confession at my first Steubenville Catholic Youth Conference.

When we got to the conference, I remember walking in and being blown away. The lights, the ambience, the big posters, and super cool flashing hashtag on the big screen: #SteubieWest #LifeTeen. It was honestly like a dream come true. I was just so energized by all of it.

The night opened with worship, and I awkwardly sang. It was the first time I had seen teens with their hands lifted in the air praising God. Sometimes, the music ministry would just let all of us sing and the music would go silent; it literally sounded like the voices of angels filling the air. It sounded so perfect.

I made a decision to go to Confession that night. I only went because I wanted to get it over with and because it was a habit for me to go before any retreat. That first Confession lasted about five minutes. Little did I know that soon I was going to learn that I had been confessing wrong for my whole life!

The next day we heard a speaker from the television show *America's Next Top Model*, Leah Darrow. Her conversion experience involved a coming home to God through the Sacrament of Confession.

She said, “The priest told me to drop the first biggest sin and go from there. So I did it, I dropped my first biggest sin. I said everything I had ever done by name and it felt amazing.”

I thought to myself, “*I’ve been hiding behind my sins... I’ve been saying what I did wrong so indirectly, and I’ve even left out sins at times, too. There are so many things I’ve done by myself and with others that I’ve never confessed because I was afraid.*”

So I went to Confession a second time. #ImBack #RoundTwo #DealWithItSatan

“Father, look,” I said. “I went to Confession yesterday, and I just realized that I’ve been leaving stuff out of Confession for so long, things that have taken place since I was little and I’m ashamed of them. I know sins are forgiven if you innocently forget to mention them in Confession, but I didn’t forget these, I just never said them and I need to say them now...” He told me to go ahead.

I sat there, my hands cold and sweaty. A few minutes passed by and I said, “Father, I’m sorry, it’s just... it’s just – this is so hard. I’m so embarrassed about what I’ve done, and you’re not going to believe it.”

He then said, “I’ve heard Confessions of prisoners in jail, I don’t think it can be that bad. God’s mercy is something so great and powerful. I’m not here to judge you.”

“Okay,” I said. I then told him I had sinned against purity. That I struggled with an attraction toward men. That I did lustful things with myself because I found myself attractive, and it was hard to not lust because what I was avoiding looking at was a part of my own body! I told him that I committed sexual sins with my male neighbor who was also the same age as me. I told him how I searched for sexual encounters over the internet that would be anonymous. I told him how I had sent explicit pictures of myself to guys. I told him everything. And I told him how I was so sorry and felt so ashamed because I’ve held these secrets in for so long. I don’t exactly remember what he said after that, but I could see in his brown eyes that he looked at me with love, and he said it was going to be okay. He told me about a ministry called *Courage*. This ministry is specifically for men and women who struggle with same-sex attractions (whether they were publicly open about their attractions or not) and who desire to grow in deeper relationship with Christ. He said to look into it because it would help me a lot.

Then he said, "I absolve you of your sins. In the name of the Father, and of the Son, and of the Holy Spirit."

As I got up and began to leave, I had a smile I could not control force its way onto my face. I was so happy. My soul felt so clean, wiped away of all my offenses. That was the first time I had ever experienced the true and beautiful reality of the sacred Sacrament of Confession. This whole time I wondered why I kept fading away from the arms of God so quickly, and it was because of mortal sins that I would purposely leave out of my Confession. The grip of sin no longer had its heavy guilt weighing down on me anymore. My heart felt so free. That Confession was the first time I admitted out loud to anybody that I was attracted to guys. I was 17 years old, and all I knew was that I wanted to eliminate all sorts of sin out of my life – particularly lustful fantasies and addictions.

As I returned to the conference, we began praise and worship. The lyrics to one song said,

"Our God is greater
Our God is stronger
God, you are higher than any other
Our God is healer
Awesome in power
Our God, our God."

(*Our God,* by Chris Tomlin)

And it was at that moment I felt God began to massively move within my heart, He began to reach into the deepest parts of my heart and cut things out that didn't belong there. Then the drums began to pick up the tempo; the beat got louder and louder, and my heart began to race. *"And if our God is for us, then who could ever stop us, and if our God is with us then what can stand against?"*

As the song progressed, I began to cry. I tried so hard not to break down in the crowd of people around me, but God's healing power was too strong for me to stand against... and it was at that moment I felt God tell me that He has been there since the beginning. He's been there at the moment of my birth, He's sorry I had to go through the bullying, through the pain of being made fun of and rejected, but He's always been there, and although I feel at times like the weight of the world is too much for me to bear, although I feel like nobody truly accepts me, I can do all things through Him. He's been there, and always will be. He told me there's no need to be afraid anymore. Like the song said, if our God is for us, then who or what can stand against us? No principality, no evil, no sin, nothing can ever stand against our God.

After praise and worship, the priest for the weekend was giving a talk about the sacrificial love of Jesus. He said, "I don't know if you struggle with lust. I don't know if you struggle with pornography. I don't know if you struggle with masturbation. Maybe you've had an abortion, or maybe you struggle with same-sex attractions. I don't know if you struggle with materialism, greed, or jealousy. Maybe you cut yourself so you can just feel something because you feel so numb. The Lord sees all of that. He sees all that brokenness, and our sin doesn't prevent Him from going to the cross, but our sin is the *reason* that He goes to the cross, and *through it* rises to new life. And so St. Paul says, "God shows His love for us in that while we were yet sinners Christ died for us. (Romans 5:8)." Later on he finally said, "And I want to tell you what love looks like. It's a man's face, and He has a crown of thorns pushed down, and there's blood coming down His face and He has one eye blacked out, and His nerve endings are on fire because of the nails in His hands holding Him to the wood. And if you were to make eye contact with Jesus at that point, what you would see in His face is that He's satisfied. He's satisfied because He's dying for you."

I sat back in my seat with glossy eyes staring at the crucifix up on stage. I was astounded. I had just admitted to a priest earlier that I was attracted to men, and I had just dropped all the weight of my sins onto Jesus' arms for Him to wash away. The beauty of the crucifixion seeped into my heart... just to know that Jesus accepted this treatment and was satisfied, it set my heart on fire. What a moving thing for somebody to do for me, to die for me. I was mesmerized by who Jesus Christ was, who He is, and who He will forever be.

Soon after that, we prepped for Eucharistic Adoration. I had been in a Eucharistic procession once before, but what was about to happen was something I did not expect. The priest walked out with the beautiful monstrance and altar servers in front of him in a procession. The smoke from the incense bathed the Eucharist and the area surrounding it. I saw, for the first time in my life, teens with their hands raised toward Jesus in the Eucharist. It looked absolutely beautiful. It looked like an ocean of people rising and falling as soon as Jesus came closer to them in the monstrance. I broke down crying again, and fell to my knees with my hands over my heart and released the pain of being called gay and being treated so harshly by my peers when I was a kid. I let it flow right out. I let my tears run in front of my God, my sweet Jesus; the only Man who has ever seen every part of who I am, with the same-sex attraction, with the addictions, and with my genuine love for Him. The Messiah whom I desired so much, fully present in the Eucharist. He made Himself known to me in a very real and powerful way that night, as He did for thousands of other teens too.

After the conference was over the next day, I felt so renewed. I had never felt so whole in my life, *ever*. It was all because of Him. I had helped on numerous retreats, and saw many lives changed, but God used that weekend to tell me, "I'm not finished with you yet." He is never really finished with us, just like He told me the very first time I encountered Him when I was in 7th grade.

8

SURFACING THE TRUTH

I came into my senior year on fire for God, and with an uncontainable joy. But I began to see many other Catholics I knew slip away from the faith. I just didn't get it, especially after witnessing so much in my past. I knew that He was real even though He surpassed our understanding. It tore my heart apart to see people I loved begin to disbelieve. It also tore me apart to see so many other teens leave the Catholic Church to go to other Christian denominations because of "better music" and services that were not "boring." I was like "What? The Catholic Mass is boring? Do you not know what the Eucharist is? Or what it means? Or how Christ is present in the sacraments?"

After my own experiences with the sacraments, I was so confused about why these people were leaving. I prayed for them because I wanted them to experience Christ in a way that you can only find in the Catholic Church. I myself, on the other hand, was in pursuit of finding answers to prove God's existence scientifically, deepening my knowledge about my own Catholic faith, and surfacing the truth of my own sexuality.

The first time I fell back into the sin of masturbation and pornography after the conference, I went to the Sacrament of Confession. I began to immerse myself in the Sacraments of Confession and Holy Communion as often as I could. A priest once told me the Catholic Church offers medicine – the frequent use of the sacraments. During my senior year, it was those two sacraments that helped me to sustain my fire. I worked toward continually deepening my love for God, even if that meant going to the Sacrament of Confession two or three times a week if it was necessary. I didn't want to be immersed in mortal sin anymore, better yet, I didn't want to be in *any* sin anymore. I wanted to *continually* be in a state of grace.

I began to consistently go to youth group, and the best thing that happened that year was when our head youth coordinator started allowing youth group to have Eucharistic Adoration for 20 minutes at the end of each youth night. I felt like a kid excited to see Jesus in the Eucharist every Monday night.

As I managed to find answers, and weed out many sins like pride, jealousy, and hate, I also realized that I was *still* addicted to pornography and lusting over men. It was very frustrating for me as an 18-year-old because I couldn't seem to narrow down what caused me to be attracted to men. Was I born like this? Was it because I didn't have much attention from my dad when I was little? Was it my longing for brotherhood? I spent numerous hours on the internet researching how same-sex attractions start, looking for success stories of re-orientation of a human's sexuality, and above all, seeing if God managed to help people stop being gay. Once I accepted the fact that I was attracted to guys, I wanted to change my orientation so badly. I didn't want to be this way. *I felt like being sexually attracted to guys meant I wasn't fully a man.* I felt like I was impaired in some way, and I was stuck in this deep constriction of trying to be chaste. Being chaste felt so much harder for me because I was exposed to guys bodies in a way many girls wouldn't know unless they were guys. I didn't want to struggle with having lustful eyes.

I knew deep down in my heart that God loved me no matter what, but I didn't want to experience these attractions. I know that it takes a male and a female to procreate and raise a family, and to give a child the opportunity to have both a mother and a father, and that that is a sacred union. I didn't want to be alone for the rest of my life, and I didn't want to date a guy. I refused to live with a guy and adopt kids. I was also afraid of "coming out" because I didn't want guys to treat me differently. I thought coming out would mean that my guy friends could no longer feel 100 percent comfortable changing around me, or even having me sleep over. I didn't want to be excluded and treated like a foreign species with a disability. I just cannot put anything else into words other than I felt deep down in my heart that I didn't want to be like this. However, I did have some peace from the realization of the truth that my attraction to men was not my identity. I realized I didn't even like calling myself "gay" because my attraction is just one part of the complex person I am. The most important identity I have is that I am God's son. Whatever struggles, attractions, or sins I also deal with – those don't define me.

At school, I was all smiles. Not one soul could have guessed I had all this confusion going on in the back of my mind. Football season had finally started, and although I had a heavy course load for a senior, I was pretty happy.

May I just say – that season for varsity football was amazing. In football, the team develops a strong brotherly bond. It felt so good to be a part of fraternal love like that. Some of my coaches cared so much for us, and the guys I was around genuinely cared about me. All this pure, brotherly love from guys helped my attractions decrease substantially. I really felt like God had a hand in blessing my senior year for me.

Senior night came toward the end of that season. To start off the football game, my team prayed the "Our Father" in the locker room. Although none of us were near perfect, it felt great to pray with my brothers. During half time, my family, and my teammates and all their families, had the opportunity to all walk together down on the field under the Friday night lights. It was a bittersweet moment. "*I'm going to miss this so much*," I thought. I was going to miss it because I had a very authentic love for those guys. To them I was just some normal guy who loved God, but on the inside I was still bearing the cross of experiencing same-sex attractions and little did they know that their genuine, loyal friendship and authentic love for me had helped my lustful attractions reduce significantly. It helped me so much to look at guys as more than just bodies; these were people with emotions, families, and souls. I really can't put into words how immense my appreciation was for those guys, and at the center of my heart I felt God just exploding in my soul. He was fulfilling my desire to belong. And it was at that moment that I realized that every person – no matter their attractions – just needs to be loved. I realized that friendships are meant to be important, even when we place God first in our lives, and that's why rejection from our peers is hurtful. I learned that brotherhood was what I *needed*, whether I experience same-sex attraction or not! The same goes for girls; they need their sisters. Coming back to reality, I looked at all the beautiful faces of not my friends, but my brothers, and thanked God for the blessing of coming into contact with all the guys I did that year for football.

Toward the end of my senior year, I applied to a medical program at the university I wanted to attend. I'm a last minute kind of guy, so I started and finished the application the day of the deadline... fortunately, I got in! I decided to tell my youth minister, Laura. I wanted to share the excitement about my application and acceptance to the program, but I also wanted to tell her more than that. I wanted to talk to her about my attraction toward guys. I needed someone's help in overcoming my lustful sins.

She met me one night because I told her I needed to talk. She bought me Starbucks, and we met at my parish and talked right outside the Eucharistic Chapel.

"Laura, look.... I am... I struggle with..." it took me nearly 15 minutes to spit the truth out. "I'm attracted to guys. I know you'd never believe it because I've dated girls before, you've seen my posts on Instagram about the girls I've taken to homecoming, but I just like guys. I wish I didn't though. My heart draws me to guys, but my mind wants to be straight. It's just so confusing and I don't even know what to think of myself. None of my friends know, my family doesn't know... just Sister Maria and the priest I confessed this to at the Steubenville Conference. But I'm also telling you this because I want to stop watching porn. Lent is coming up and I want to get this out of my life. So there's this website called Covenant Eyes, and it monitors everything you watch and sends somebody reports of what you view on the internet. I was wondering if you could get those emails so I can be held accountable. It costs $10 a month and I'm not working anymore right now, but I'll manage to save up some lunch money to pay for it."

She looked at me with watery eyes and said, "Okay, okay I'll get the emails."

I went to Mass every morning for Lent that year at 6:30 a.m. I also went to Confession every week and Eucharistic Adoration as much as I could. I didn't totally eliminate my addiction to porn, but I reduced it significantly. I used to watch it multiple times a day, every day of the week. But after Lent I reduced it to as little as once a week. That was a huge deal for me. I wanted to stop this sin.

I also decided to tell my best friend Nick about my attraction to guys. Nick is that one friend you've known for only a few years, but he knows everything about you. He was also a good man of God and loved being Catholic. In fact, he was in the seminary during that spring of my senior year.

I couldn't sleep the night I was going to tell him. It was 3:00 a.m. and I was feeling so ugly about myself because I hated the way I felt toward men. I hated that I couldn't control what I desired and could not get it fixed. I had gone to counseling already, and I felt like it was just no use. I felt like I should have just seen a psychologist to see what he or she could do. My thoughts went as far as thinking that maybe I just need an exorcism to drive out this attraction. I felt so desperate, and I was so frustrated with this attraction and I just needed a brother to lean on.

I sent him a text message and said, "Hey brotha, are you up?"

He quickly replied, "Actually yeah I am, what's up?"

"Can I come over to talk? There's just something I need to tell you."

"Okay, come over bro."

I pulled up outside his house in my dad's truck. Orange street lights flooded his house and the trees standing by it.

"What's up man?" he said.

"Okay look dude, I don't know exactly how to say this..." I sat there in the car with him for an even longer time than I did with Laura just trying to get it out of my mouth. "Okay, well, I'm not going to exactly say what it is. I'm going to talk about my childhood and try to explain why I think I may be what I am..." I went onto explain everything I had researched and all that I was trying to figure out on my own about being attracted to members of my gender. "... and, Nick, well..." my hands were clammy, and my heart was racing, "I'm attracted to guys, Nick... and I can't control it either."

After I said that I couldn't even bare to look at him in the eyes. I just stared out into the darkness of the street with my eyes beginning to swell with tears. I then looked down at my hands and thought, "*I'm such a mess.*"

"Dude," he said, "I'm sorry you feel so ugly about yourself. What I see in front of me is someone who needs love. But man, you're not a bad person because of who you are attracted to! A priest once told me that you can't control if a bird flies over your head, but you can control if it lays a nest on your head. I'm not going to look at you any differently. Just remember that. You are still a beloved son of God, and that's all that matters. I love you, man."

I felt so relieved that I had a brother who finally could hear me out. I had a man who I could lean on, a man whose brotherhood was founded on Christ. I love that guy so much.

9

MY FATHER'S HOUSE

The summer after I graduated high school left me feeling disillusioned. It was bittersweet. I knew that I was going to move onto bigger and better things, but I also knew I was going to miss some of the friends that I made.

Although I was definitely pleased that God had finally given me a group of brothers who I could call my close friends, I quickly noticed that they became my ultimate treasure, rather than God. I realized that I was longing for deep intimacy that my friends could not satisfy. I noticed that even my friends weren't truly happy. I mean we were glad to have each other, but they also longed for something more than just each other's friendship. After much contemplation, I came to the conclusion that we were also longing for God. I knew it was exactly that because I had been in church communities where Christ was the center of our lives, and our friendships always seem to be filled with radiant joy.

I recognized that I was placing my hope and joy solely on my friends; on earthly things rather than my Creator. I knew that I needed to go to another Steubenville Conference that year to re-center my desires and enter into a deeper communion with my Father. And in addition to that, I was attending Franciscan LEAD that year. (LEAD is a leadership retreat that takes place a couple of days before the actual conference.) My prayer heading into that week was, "*God, I just know that I want more of You, and I know that I've placed other things before You, but all I really want is You.*"

Franciscan LEAD and the Steubenville Youth Conference was the first time in my life that I had the opportunity to encounter God as my Father. And I knew that although I lacked a lot of love and affection from my dad as a kid, my Father up in heaven was ready and waiting to fulfill my longing for authentic fatherhood. He came to my rescue because I cried out to Him; a desperate call for my Dad. And He knew that I just longed for healing from all the pain that same-sex attractions had brought me. I wanted to heal from all the internal distress brought about because of my struggle, which felt like an ocean of chaos. I was tired of not feeling deeply close to other good Catholic guys because I felt they wouldn't understand my suffering if I told them I experience same-sex attractions. God knew how badly I prayed that He would take this cross from me.... *He knew I didn't want this anymore*. I was tired of feeling so ugly about myself because I felt a way that I couldn't control.

One of the nights on Franciscan LEAD, we had the opportunity to pray in total silence. It was that night that I felt God the Father embrace me in the stillness of my heart. He spoke so loudly to me, without any music, without any people, in the quiet of my soul. And all God was trying to tell me was that it's going to be all right. He knew that I had placed other things above Him in my life, but it was going to be okay! *He loved me, anyway.* As a good Father does whenever his kid begins to go astray, He gently calls His son back with love. Whenever we run away, He doesn't wait with fury for us to return. He stands there missing us.

Like the story of the Prodigal Son (Luke 15:11-32), our Father stands watching and waiting for us to come back. In this story, a father has two sons. One day, the father's younger son asks his dad for all of his inheritance. He takes the money his father gives him and wastes it on parties and women. But the moment this son realizes he can't find his self-worth and true fulfillment in these things, he gets up and goes home to his father. As the son walks back home, he is scared to see his dad. "*What is he going to say when I get home?*" he wonders. The second the father's son sets foot on the property line, the father takes off, sprinting toward him. And this is exactly what God made me realize. When we're gone, He looks at the dinner table at the very spot we used to sit and eat at and He thinks, "Gosh, how I *miss* my child." He goes to our room and looks at our closet and says, "How I miss his beautiful face, and his free spirit living his life as he is." The father just wants us to return as we are, even if we feel we are at the messiest points in our lives. The thing is this: *He just wants us in His arms*. That's exactly what I felt that night – that I was wrapped up in my Father's arms. As a little boy, that's all I wanted from my dad, that sort of physical and emotional intimacy. All we want as humans is pure and holy intimacy, and I realized that if intimacy is something we lack in our lives, Jesus can *fill those longings*, He can and will fill those voids.

When the day of the actual conference arrived, I was so stoked. That night, the worship for me was unforgettable. It felt *amazing* to be with other Catholics again who love God as much as I do and to pray and praise together with them.

"Holy Spirit You are welcome here
Come flood this place and fill the atmosphere
Your glory God is what our hearts long for
To be overcome by Your Presence, Lord"

(*Holy Spirit*, by Bryan & Katie Torwalt)

As worship continued, I could feel my soul being elevated by the music. My eyes were filled to the brim with tears ready to burst forth as we were led deeper into the mantra of "Holy Spirit." My heart literally rejoiced in God my Savior, and I could feel myself being elevated into a communion with God that I simply cannot put into words. During every prayer after that, I lifted my hands up toward heaven like a little kid who wanted to be picked up by his Dad. And that's exactly how God responded to me – as my Dad. I felt like I was a 7-year-old boy just calling out to his father. And this Father didn't hound me with the question or whether or not I was gay, but rather, He just embraced me as His son. That was enough for Him.

"I hear the Savior say,
'Thy strength indeed is small;
Child of weakness, watch and pray,
Find in Me thine all in all.'"

(*Jesus Paid It All*, by Elvina M. Hall)

During adoration, the priest processed around the room, and he stopped right in front of me with the monstrance. I was on my feet reaching out to Him, my Jesus. I fell to my knees in bitter tears. Many people knew me on the outside as this always happy, super religious kid up until that point, and I was so tired of putting on a happy face acting like everything was okay, as if I had nothing tough going on in my life. People thought I was perfect, and that my home life was perfect, but it wasn't. So I let my broken self come out of hiding in front of my Savior as His son. My heavenly Father didn't judge me for who I was or what I struggled with. I was slumped over the chair in front of me just crying. In that moment, I knew two things: 1) God has given me the opportunity to truly see the wounds on His side and His hands. God is *real*, beyond a doubt. 2) He reached out to me in the way I needed Him, and in the way that He really is, as my Savior. My God saves!

10

FOREVER ALONE?

I wish I could say that I was a completely perfect son of God after that conference, but unfortunately I was not. What that conference kicked off for me was the upheaval and realization of my restlessness with same-sex attraction. It was time to begin to let the unrest go. I wish I could have managed to maintain the same amount of zeal I had after the conference, but the reality of single life eventually hit me like a load of bricks.

I started off my first semester of college burnt out from high school. I wanted to hold on tightly to my friends from before, and I didn't want life to change. Although many of my friends went to the college I went to, it felt like a lonely world because school was demanding a whole bunch of our time and effort.

Lacking a deeply knit social community, a sense of desolation began to take a firm grip on me. With all this time to think about my life by myself, I also began to wonder, "*Does the fact I'm attracted to other guys mean I'm called to be single forever?* Does this mean that I have to live alone?" This is where my faith journey took a terrible turn.

I became angry with God. I was mad at Him. I thought, "*I know God exists... I know He loves me... and I know the Catholic Church contains the fullness of the truth and is the great mother Church where Jesus makes Himself fully present... but why am I struggling with this? And why doesn't God take this away?*" I was consistent with my frequent visits to the Blessed Sacrament in Adoration, going to Mass, and receiving the Sacrament of Confession. Yet God still wouldn't take the struggle away. I felt like I was doing my part, so why wasn't God doing His?

I asked countless priests about what I should do because I wanted this orientation to go away. I wanted to maybe meet a woman of great faith and love for God to captivate me and change me. It was tough because some of the answers I got made me feel worse.

I became furious with God because I didn't purposely choose celibacy. I didn't want to be celibate. I didn't want to live alone. I thought, "*Certain men that are called to priesthood respond to God and are willing to give up married life. Why don't I have a choice? Straight men who become priests had an opportunity to date and experience what intimate love is like with a significant other. I can't experience that because it's wrong and because the way I want to act out is contrary to God's plan for our sexuality.*"

I yearned for a boyfriend. So, I rebelled against God and the rules I felt were so cruelly being forced on me. I began to seek out romantic encounters with other males. I didn't know how else to manage my attractions. I wanted to be free from doing these things, but I also craved sexual intimacy, even lustful intimacy, and I was tired of having these unsatisfied desires.

I thought, "*If other straight, Catholic guys can go crazy and give into sexual sin, and come back to God with mercy, why can't I go crazy?*" In reality, this was totally the wrong way to go about things. Everyone is called to chastity, and it is just as wrong for a straight guy to "go crazy" as it was for me.

One night, I planned to get together with another friend who I knew experienced same-sex attractions and was feeling low about it too. When I drove over to his house, my heart began to race, and I had a sick feeling in my stomach. Part of me wanted to give into what I thought would be fulfilling and another part of me wanted to turn away from sin altogether. I wish I could say that the good half of me won in that moment. But I was angry with God, and that anger fueled my desire to sin. I thought, "*This is what you get God. So be it. You won't take this struggle away.*"

As I pulled up to his house, he got in my car, and we drove off. We did things that I knew my body wanted but in the middle of everything, I could feel my conscience crying out to me, "stop, just please, please stop." I stopped what I was doing and told him,

"Dude, this is wrong. We can't do this anymore. You're supposed to be my brother, my friend. This is just so wrong..." After we got back to his house, I didn't know what else to do but pray, so I asked him, "Bro, do you mind if we pray? I just can't deal with this right now, I feel so terrible about what we did." He agreed, and I asked God to forgive us for what we had done, and I apologized that I even gave consent to such a thing.

When I drove home, I had never felt so full of disgust with myself. *"I don't know anymore, God,"* I thought. Strictly speaking, I hadn't lost the gift of physical virginity, because that was one thing I knew I always wanted to keep, even if I was never going to get married. That winter, I ended up helping on another Teen A.C.T.S. retreat as a young adult. As I looked at all the teens coming off that retreat, I could see the Lord beautifully burning in their hearts. When I saw the love they had for each other and for me, I thought, *"Fighting the good fight is worth it. Even though I don't know how things are going to play out, it's just better altogether stop myself from freely giving into lustful desires."*

After that retreat, with the help of God, I managed to break my addiction to porn, and the longing for these lustful encounters reduced significantly. But as my desires purified, my longing for a partner didn't go away. I wanted a boyfriend. I wanted somebody to hold in my arms; just the way a good, Catholic, straight guy longs to hold his beautiful girlfriend in his arms in a pure and holy way. Out of my own curiosity, I searched for a guy to date. I thought it would be okay because I wasn't looking for a guy to have sex with, I only wanted a pure relationship. I don't know what made me think that was okay, but I justified it.

I ended up meeting a really nice guy who was also like me; he came off as straight to everybody but deep down was attracted to guys. We started talking, and I connected with him. It felt good to be wanted, known, and loved by another person. It felt good to let myself be open to this guy's affection and compliments. Despite the fact that the stage we were in was simply flirting with each other, I still felt like I was living in sin! I knew I wasn't doing anything dirty with this guy, but I still felt guilty.

I had become so fed up with being attracted to guys, that every time I looked at a happy straight couple, my heart filled with deep hate and jealousy. *"You guys don't know how lucky you are to be straight,"* I cynically thought. I began to backfire at everybody in my life – my family, my parents, my Catholic friends. I became so angry. "*Why God? Why me?*"

With all these different emotions and with a deeply constricted heart, I went out for a run late at night. The orange street lamps dropped their spotlights in intervals over the street ahead of me. I put on my headphones, and all I could listen to was Christian music; I didn't have anything else on my phone. As I ran, I didn't even feel like hearing that kind of music. I was filled with disgust toward God. Then one song came on with words that seemed to seep their way into my heart. It was *Forever Reign* by One Sonic Society.

"And Oh, I'm running to Your arms, I'm running to Your arms."

Running across the streets that night, I discreetly wiped "sweat" from my face when in reality I was trying to hide the fact that I wanted to break down and that I was starting to cry. I felt bad for letting something like this attraction bother me this much. I knew there were bigger problems out there in the world other than my own sexual orientation. I wish I had also known then that every heartache is important in the eyes of God, no matter how petty or small it seems to be.

On a Friday afternoon, I called up my youth ministers, David and Hannah, almost crying because I couldn't keep the frustration of this struggle to myself anymore. I needed to vent what was on my mind. I told the married couple I wanted to tell my parents that I experience same-sex attraction. I was tired of feeling alone in my struggle, and I needed my parents' love and support to live out a good Catholic faith in the situation I was in.

The next day I went to the Sacrament of Confession, and I told the priest that although my heart desires to be with a man as my husband, I'd rather have a complete love and deep relationship with God. I didn't want to give up my faith over one part of life that I couldn't partake in. I was happier that way. I also told him that I was talking to a guy with the intention of having him as my pure, chaste partner, but I felt guilty. I knew God was telling me in my heart that this just wasn't right. I knew that the right way for me to live would be chastely single. For the first time in my life, I was at peace with that reality. I was happy with what God ultimately called somebody like me to do (as He calls every person to do) – live my Catholic faith chastely.

I'm now 19 years old. I've managed to talk to my mom about my struggle, and I can clearly see how God had a huge hand in the way things turned out. She loves me and supports me in my call to a chaste, celibate life. We're still praying about how to tell my sister and father. There is no doubt though that sooner or later, they'll know. That's only because I love them, and they mean the world to me, and I want to share a personal part of myself with them.

One night, when I was up late thinking, one of the two best friends I have from high school football, Jose, texted me asking if I was all right. I managed to tell him everything, and one of the best things I heard him say was, "What made you ever think I'd stop being your friend after this? You're my boy!" With the help of Jose, I also managed to also tell my other best friend Ben that I experience same-sex attractions. I was so afraid that they were going to stop talking to me altogether after that but, crazy enough, it was through me telling them about my struggle that our friendship and brotherly bond grew so much deeper. I could now be 100 percent honest with them about myself. I was able to tell them how much I felt burdened, and the fact I could express myself and my trials with them gave me the deep brotherhood I needed from other males. There was no more hiding. Telling people in my life who mean so much to me about this part of me feels so liberating, and it allowed me to rest emotionally for once.

Believe it or not, I have some younger brothers and sisters in Christ tell me at times that they look up to me and want to grow spiritually alongside me. I never felt worthy of being a "spiritual older brother," but for whatever reason God wants me to be there. And even though I experience same-sex attractions, God has helped me realize that He wants to use all of us for His greater glory, despite our struggles.

If there's anything I've learned in this whole process of figuring out who I am, it's that I need to stop trying to figure myself out. I need to remember that above any orientation, above the sports we're in, above the grades we get, above the clubs were a part of, above our social status, we are ultimately just sons and daughters of God. We are all trying to find a place in this world, and we are looking for meaning that really can only be filled by Christ. My heart has become so at peace with that realization. I am a beloved son of God, and that is all that matters. Now, when I drive to school, interact with friends, go running, lead worship at my church, talk to my youth group, I rest in peace knowing that I am a son of God.

I don't know what's going to happen in my life, but I know that God has never failed me before in my other struggles, and He won't start now. I'm just going to trust in what He's got planned for me.

My life isn't perfect, but that doesn't mean I don't love living it. I think God has a really nice way of turning broken hearts into the most joyfully mended souls. I know the best thing I can do with my life is to live deeply in love with my Father; after all, living your life for Him can't even be properly described with the word fulfilling because God transcends *beyond* that. I'm in pursuit of the King of my heart, and I want to live this adventure with Him. I know I'll be happy with Him as my main man. It may not be easy... but in the end ultimately everything will be okay because He's looking out for me. I once heard someone say, "*I don't know what my future holds, but I know who holds my future.*"

The biggest thing God has told me in all of this is that it's not my fault I struggle with attractions toward guys. What God is now doing is simply teaching me to deeply love *myself and who I am*; a boy made with love, created to love and to be united with Christ. No matter what, I'm redeemed. And so are *YOU*. Whether you are gay, straight, or somewhere in between, Christ loves you and longs for you and has been in pursuit of your heart long before you began pursuing HIs. And He has no intention of ever stopping.

Q&A

CATHOLIC ANSWERS TO COMMON QUESTIONS

CHAPTER 1:

Can you "become gay" by the power of persuasion by someone saying you're gay at a young age like AJ's dad did?

There are a lot of differing opinions and studies that have been done on how a person comes to experience same-sex attractions. The Catechism of the Catholic Church states that as far as same-sex attractions go, the "psychological genesis remains largely unexplained" (CCC 2357). A variety of factors may be present within a person that cause him or her to experience same-sex attraction. For some people, there may be psychological wounds from the past that need healing, for others there may be a deeper "psychological genesis," that they may never discover.

It is very important to remember that, regardless of "why" a person experiences same-sex attraction, every person was created by God to become a saint. The Church offers a path for everyone, regardless of their struggle toward holiness. AJ may not fully understand how his attractions surfaced, but he does have a choice how he lives his life moving forward.

Is it offensive to ask someone if they are gay?

Yes. It is offensive to ask someone if they are gay for multiple reasons. First of all, by asking that question you are defining them or characterizing them by something (their sexual attractions) that is only one facet of the complexity of who they are as a person.

Secondly, it is rude to ask someone if they are gay because they have no obligation to talk about their sexual attractions and divulge that private information to anyone.

Lastly, asking someone "are you gay?" often comes across as an accusation, sometimes forcing that person to make a declaration or claim on an identity. Further, this sends the wrong message because we never want anyone to feel that they are less important, less precious, or less loved because of the attractions they experience. We are called to treat every person in a way that recognizes his or her inherent dignity (CCC 2358). And it goes without saying that if it would be inappropriate to ask the person if they are gay, it would be even more inappropriate to ask others if that person is gay. Get to know the person, enter into conversation about appropriate things, and allow the Lord to strengthen the relationship without gossip or crossing boundaries.

What should I do if I feel like don't fit into "manly" activities as a boy, or "girly" activities as a girl?

It's totally fine if you don't feel like you can thrive in certain activities that are more geared toward your sex. Jesus said that He came, "that they may have life and have it abundantly" (John 10:10). God gave you gifts and talents that will help your soul to feel alive. Sometimes, we equate "masculinity" to things like being a great football star or femininity to things like being able to dance or sing well. Our masculinity and femininity run much deeper than activities we choose to do. As AJ learns, what it means to "be a man" wasn't related to how well he played football, it related to his identity as an adopted son of God.

You are enough, just as you are. If you feel like you're being forced into an activity that doesn't suit you, it may be time to have an honest conversation with your parents to let them know that you'd like to have the freedom to find out what sports and/or extracurricular activities will be a better fit for who you are. It never helps to lie to yourself and try to force yourself to do something that isn't life-giving. On the other hand, if you are feeling a struggle fitting in with people of the same sex, maybe this is an opportunity to step into the discomfort and try a new activity. Our sex does not have to define our activities or friends, but be open to trying. It is important that we develop strong, chaste friendships with people of the same and the opposite sex.

CHAPTER 2:

What is lust?

Lust is defined as "disordered desire for or inordinate enjoyment of sexual pleasure. Sexual pleasure is morally disordered when sought for itself, isolated from its procreative and unitive purposes" (CCC 2351). So in other words, it means to desire sexual pleasure purely for the pleasure of it apart from the biological and spiritual function of union and procreation between a husband and wife.

Why is lust wrong? Isn't that just called "being attracted to someone"?

Lust is a sin because besides simply being attracted to someone, it means you desire sexual pleasure in and of itself. If love is a self-gift for the good of another, lust is the opposite: Lust is totally self-interested and seeks only the good of one's self. Lust always occurs when we separate sex from marriage, even if we convince ourselves that we are not lusting over our partner. Lust can also occur within marriages, though, especially if one spouse begins to selfishly desire the other only for sex. God created sexual intercourse and sexual activities that lead toward intercourse to be experienced in a loving union between a man and a woman in order to unite them and bring about children (CCC 1604). These are the two purposes of sex (union and procreation) and they can only happen properly and fully within an opposite-sex marriage. To separate the two purposes of sex is to degrade it and make it something different than what it was designed to be. It turns it into a lie and something that is no longer creative, but destructive to us spiritually, emotionally, and sometimes physically. Lust is a sin because it buys into the lie that our selfish desire tells us, "you can use someone for pleasure, for fantasy." When we believe and act upon that lie, we not only destroy the dignity of another person, but we destroy ours, as well.

If I experience same-sex attraction how do I protect myself from the temptation of lust when I'm in a situation like AJ in the locker room?

There are occasions of sin that we can avoid, and then there are temptations that are going to be part of our lives no matter what we do. Being aware that temptation is normal, and that it's not a sin to feel tempted, is an important part of your spiritual growth. If you over-focus on trying to not feel tempted, this can actually increase temptation by directing your mind toward it. It's like, if someone says, "Don't think about an elephant," suddenly you're thinking about elephants. Satan wants you to take every one of his temptations seriously because he wants to be the center of your universe. Instead, when the temptation comes, acknowledge it, name it in your head, and offer it to God and ask Him to purify your thoughts and feelings. Then try to turn your attention to other things. If you can't stop looking, try to make it an occasion of grace rather than an occasion of sin. Give thanks for the beauty of the body, and ask for the grace to appreciate that beauty without lust. Keep learning about the dignity of the human person, and ask God to help you see everyone as brothers and sisters and not objects that you can use to give your mind and body pleasure. Above all, cooperate with grace patiently: purification of thoughts and desires is a long process and there's nothing you can do to make it happen overnight.

How can you be friends with someone of the same sex who is "gay" and potentially attracted to you?

Just because a person experiences same-sex attraction, that doesn't mean they're attracted to every single person of their sex. So how do you be friends with them? The same way you would be friends with anyone else. A person's sexual attractions is not a reason for you to treat them differently. In fact, having a regular friendship with them may be the best way to help them integrate into appropriate, chaste relationships with people of both sexes.

CHAPTER 3:

How do I let God into my life like AJ did on retreat?

God wants nothing more than to be in your life. The question is if you'll be open enough to allow Him to love you. If you're going on a retreat, go with no expectations. Don't compare your experience to other retreats you've been on. Don't look at what God is doing in other people's lives. Be completely present. Stop worrying about the outside world. Don't overthink. Don't spend the whole time on your phone. And most importantly, pray for openness.

What if I don't feel anything when I pray?

That's okay. You won't always feel something when you pray. That's not always how God works and that's not the purpose of prayer. We can pray to ask for God's grace. We can pray to intercede for other people. We can pray to grow deeper in our relationship with God. Sometimes when God seems to be silent, He's really teaching us about who He is. Even our most lofty thoughts and beautiful emotions about God aren't God, but sometimes they can become idols. We end up worshiping our feelings rather than worshiping God Himself. When we can't feel God, it's often because He's quietly leading us toward a more intense kind of intimacy with Him – but it takes time. Many of the saints experienced this and their lives serve as an example of what true, mature faith looks like.

Is it because of his faith that AJ feels guilty about his experience of same-sex attractions? Maybe that's why he was in denial?

Part of AJ's hesitation to accept that he experiences same-sex attractions was a fear of what others would think, and whether or not his friends, family, and community would still accept and love him. The Church never wants anyone to feel like they are less important, or less worthy of love and acceptance because of the attractions they experience. This should serve as a wake up call to all of us Christians to be more vigilant in how we treat those who experience same-sex attractions, whether it is making jokes about them or gossiping about them. In order to ensure they will feel welcomed and loved by us, we need to only act with charity and not judgments of the heart or condemnations based on who we think they ought to be.

Very often "religion" and "Catholic guilt" are blamed when a person feels badly for what they have done. This is, in part, a good thing because we should absolutely feel remorse for choosing sin instead of God. This remorse can lead us to seek forgiveness and to have a deeper desire to change our ways. However, this is all only beneficial when it is in regards to our actions and choices. "Religion" or "Catholic guilt" should never make us ashamed of who we are. That is false and misguided. That is not the Gospel message. Jesus accepts each of us as we are – no matter what our race, class, and sexual attractions are. He wants us, and the whole

Church, to feel and reflect that love to others. We are beloved and accepted and affirmed by our God... but all our actions aren't, nor should they be. When we choose sin it hurts us, it hurts God, and it hurts our brothers and sisters in Christ. That shouldn't be okay with anyone... not God and not us.

CHAPTER 4:

Why is porn wrong? Doesn't almost everyone look at it?

Yes, many people look at porn. But a lot of people lie, too. Does that make it right? Of course not! Porn is objectively immoral regardless of how many people say it's normal and okay (CCC 2354). Porn is wrong because it twists, distorts, and destroys the act of sex by reducing it to entertainment. The Catechism of the Catholic Church uses the word "perverts" to describe the profound negative impact pornography has on sex (CCC 2354). It causes the person watching porn to have lustful fantasies, which takes sexual pleasure and makes it an end to be sought for itself. Also, more scientific and psychological studies are proving that porn can be as addictive as a drug, it warps the user's view of love and relationships, and it often leads to violence or the desire for violence within a sexual relationship. Porn also hurts the people who are involved in making it. These are real people who are performing sex acts – often violent or extreme sex acts – for money. It's a lot like hiring a prostitute, except that you're paying to watch someone be sexually exploited rather than paying to sexually exploit them yourself. Ultimately, porn is empty and unsatisfying in the long run and has a profound and damaging impact on our soul.

The use of pornography can also be a significant stumbling block in discerning what God wants for you in life. If you are called to marriage, priesthood, or consecrated life, it will be very difficult to discern those self-giving callings if you are regularly focused only on your selfish desires through the use of pornography. Deal with this at a young age and make a commitment to refuse to use porn so that you don't have to deal with the incredible struggles of pornography addiction later in life. If this is something you struggle with, there are lots of places to get help and free yourself from porn addiction. You can find them at TheVictoryApp.com, CovenantEyes.com, and ThePornEffect.com.

How do you witness to your friends about God, purity, and love without being made fun of?

Look at how AJ does this. He is in a great place to speak about God, purity, and love because he already had a friendship with Emma. He has gained her trust. This relationship is key to speaking hard truth. His intentions come purely from wanting the absolute best for Emma. He speaks about God courageously because that's how much he genuinely cares for her and loves God. He doesn't come off as condemning or "preachy" because he speaks with compassion and speaks to her as his friend. This is how we are all called to speak about God.

What does it mean to respect men and women in our relationships with them?

If we seek to treat men and women with respect, then we must begin by seeing women as daughters of God, and men as sons of God, all with dignity and worth because God made each of us precious and unique. He has an incredible plan for every one of us (Jeremiah 29:11). So often we degrade ourselves and others by being okay with looking at other people as a means to an end, or just seeing their worth in what they're able to do for us, or how good they are able to make us feel. This is degrading because it means treating people like tools rather than valuing the whole person, body and soul.

CHAPTER 5:

Why was AJ constantly worried about being perceived as "gay"? Why not just accept it?

AJ was worried about being perceived as "gay" because from a very young age he was taught by other people's words and actions that being "gay" is something bad, and that if you are attracted to the same sex, you are worth less than other people. He thought that others would judge him and not accept and love him. We all have different paths to walk as we journey toward knowing and loving ourselves, and that's okay. One thing is for sure though – AJ knew that his sexual attractions weren't the main thing that defined him. The Catholic Church has always emphasized that our sexual desires are a part of who we are, but it is an aspect of ourselves that does not define who we are. Basically, we can't start with our sexual desires and define ourselves. We need to start deeper. We are made as men in the image and likeness of God, and God knows us, loves us, and adopts us as sons. We are made as women in the image and likeness of God, and God knows us, loves us, and adopts us as daughters. This is the top part of our identity, and everything else gets ordered toward that reality.

Our sexuality and our sexual desires are something that are integrated into our total person; they are an important part of who we are. How we act upon them can be impacted by sin. Priests and religious brothers and sisters promise to be celibate, that is, they promise to abstain from all sexual activity and sexual/romantic relationships. They integrate their sexuality in a specific way that is different than how a married couple integrates their sexuality.

If we choose to integrate our sexuality in a way contrary to God's plan and design for it, we actually aren't integrating our sexuality at all. Integrating our sexuality (chastity) allows us to be free to love in ways that bring life, rather than hinder or destroy it.

How can God use us in our brokenness to serve Him?

God very often uses the most broken people to lead others to Him. He has a way of using our brokenness to shine through us, and make something beautiful. For example Jesus calls Matthew, a sinful tax collector, to be His disciple (Matthew 9:9-13). At the time tax collectors were seen as the lowest of the low and known for being corrupt and stealing people's money. And yet Jesus still calls Matthew to drop everything and follow Him. He can use our testimony to speak through us and to reach other people. God doesn't call the "perfect" people who think they have it all together; rather, He calls the unqualified, the sinful, and the broken. AJ kept going on retreats and helping to lead retreats and leaning in to his church community not because he was perfect, but because he was humbly seeking to know, love, and serve God.

Why are meaningful friendships and non-romantic relationships so important?

Brotherhood was so important for AJ because every single one of us is made for communion – to love and be loved by God and by other people. Any time that we become isolated from those around us, we experience loneliness and the feeling of not being fully alive. Sometimes we choose this for ourselves, and sometimes it's forced on us by the rejection of others. However, God does not want this for us, which is why the Church is so beautiful. It's a huge community of brothers and sisters in Christ, striving to live in virtue and get to heaven. In a more specific way, AJ longed for brotherhood because it's essential for young men and women to find acceptance and connection with their same sex for healthy development. We each need to know that we are accepted and loved by those who are like us. The friendships that you have with your brothers and sisters in Christ are important to them, not only emotionally and spiritually, but also for their mental development as a person. We were made for community. We were made by God to love and to be loved, with virtue at the forefront of our relationships.

CHAPTER 6

If I watch porn and find I'm attracted to the same sex does that mean I'm gay?

No. Watching a certain kind of porn is not an indication of your sexual orientation. Porn is the worst place to learn about sexuality, because at the very core pornography is a lie. Porn is a multi-billion-dollar industry that makes money by trying to get you to keep coming back for more. John Wood, a therapist who works with youth who watch porn, says, "A competitive market means that pornographers are trying to outdo each other to come up with the most extreme images, this contest to push the boundaries means that straight intercourse is considered too boring." This means gay porn or abusive porn becomes more normalized and teaches your brain to become aroused by these unrealistic, surgically altered, graphic images when you might not be otherwise.

Is it possible to "turn straight" if you experience same-sex attractions?

Sexual attraction is complicated, and it often develops over the course of a person's life. There are some people who in their past have experienced same-sex attractions, but now experience opposite sex (heterosexual) attractions. For many, as they are growing and learning more about themselves, they find that same-sex attraction fades or goes away completely and they have turned toward healthy and strong marriages with the opposite sex. However, this is not the case for everyone and people have taken a lot of different steps to get there. Many who experience same-sex attraction will have that same attraction their whole lives.

If you, or someone you know, wants to explore this, it's imperative that you understand it's not necessarily about "curing" or "fixing" something wrong with you. It's about possibly healing any deep-seated wounds from your past that may be affecting how you perceive yourself and your relationships today and how your mind, body, and soul interact with the world. Even if healing these wounds doesn't impact feelings of same-sex attraction, that doesn't mean we should be discouraged. Life is a journey of holiness, and any wound that impacts our emotional and psychological health limits us. The goal for all of us is to achieve freedom and peace, an ever-deepening union with Christ, and most importantly heaven, which is possible no matter what your attractions may be (CCC 2359). The best advice is to talk to a trusted, Catholic or Christian therapist in order to become the healthiest version of yourself in mind, body, and soul and to stay rooted in the sacraments of the Church and prayer.

Why do you feel empty when you're serving in ministry? Shouldn't doing work for God and the Church enliven you?

Many people experience feeling empty because they are constantly giving their energy, time, and emotions to their ministry. If a person is empty, or spiritually dry, they have nothing to give to others in ministry. That's why we need to spend as much time with the Lord ourselves before we can even think about helping others with their faith. It's important to remember that grace sometimes works immediately in our lives, and other times it has a gradual impact. We must be continually seeking grace so we may be continually changed and transformed by Jesus.

CHAPTER 7

How do I lay it all out like AJ did in Confession?

The first step is to understand that the priest isn't there to condemn you – he is there in place of Christ to love you and pour God's mercy and grace upon you. Priests have heard a lot Confessions, and it's likely that what you say won't take him by surprise. The second step is to do an examination of conscience, which helps you to recall your sins. If you need help, write down your sins and bring them with you into the Sacrament of Confession. And lastly know that all priests must live by the seal of Confession meaning that a priest cannot disclose anything you tell him in Confession, no matter what it is. In that moment, you are speaking to Christ directly through the priest. The priest himself doesn't have a right to the knowledge you are sharing with Christ, he is only an instrument. The priest wants nothing more than to wash you of your sins so that you can experience the healing and freedom of God's love and mercy.

Don't forget though, that priests are human and they are not perfect. It would be ideal if every priest understood how to counsel a person who experiences same-sex attractions but that is not always the case. If a priest is harsh with you, or condemning, or says something that sounds false and doesn't sit right with you, don't be afraid to talk to someone else about it and to do your own research into what the Church teaches. Try to find a priest who can be your regular confessor who will challenge you to live the Church's teaching, but who also manifests mercy, humility, and humor in his preaching and ministry. Don't let a negative Confession experience keep you away from this powerful Sacrament. God's mercy is never ending and He wants you to experience the freedom and love of His forgiveness.

I've never had an "ah-ha" or obvious "God moment" in my life. How do I have one?

Our faith should never be built on the "big signs" God gives us, nor should we wait for one. It's easy to compare what God has done in someone else's life to what He has done in yours. What we should do is believe without seeing or as the Bible says "walk by faith, not by sight." God reveals Himself in His perfect timing in a way that's personal to you. Our hearts need to be open to recognize how God makes Himself obvious to us numerous times throughout our day. Those conversion moments that come with strong emotions are rare, or for some faithful, holy Catholics – non-existent. Conversions happen constantly when you are living for God. It's not a one-time thing. Being a saint is about constantly examining our lives for ways we can grow closer to God through a life of virtue.

What is Eucharistic Adoration?

In short, Eucharistic Adoration is the adoring of Jesus Christ, fully present – Body, Blood, Soul, and Divinity – in the Eucharist. It is a period of time where we can pray and be in His holy presence. Many people use the time to be in silent prayer, but it can also be a time of singing praise and worship songs.

CHAPTER 8

Does faith make gay people hate themselves?

Unfortunately, we have to acknowledge that the way that Christian communities have treated people who experience same-sex attractions has not always been good. Sometimes it's been really bad. In AJ's story we see some of these bad behaviors: bullying, shaming, name-calling. All of these things certainly can and do contribute to a young person's feelings of self-hatred. As Christians, we need to take responsibility and apologize for doing things that make people feel that they are hated and rejected by God. Sometimes people will justify their cruelty by saying that they are defending the truth, but the greatest truth is the revelation of God's immense love for all of His people. When we tell the truth about lesser things in a way that obscures the most important thing, we are, as St. Paul says, like "clanging gongs." In AJ's case we can see that he was hurt and rejected for his sexuality before he even had any notion of what sexuality is.

That's why the Church teaches that people who experience same-sex attractions must be treated with respect and compassion. The Church's teachings on sexual morality are meant to help us to find our vocations and to live the lives that God has planned for us. They are supposed to teach us how to love more fully, and to show us the right ways to express that love. They should never become an excuse for hateful or unjust behavior.

Doesn't loving someone who experiences same-sex attractions mean we shouldn't judge them for their sexuality and how they choose to live their lives?

There are two answers to this question. First, you should never judge and condemn the heart of a person for any reason, especially not for their sexuality. We are not defined by our sexuality; we are defined by our identity as sons and daughters of God. Pray for the grace to see every person in this way first and foremost as your brother or sister in Christ. However, loving someone and seeing them as your brother or sister doesn't mean that you can or should condone whatever actions they choose. If you knew that a loved one was doing something that was harmful to them (in either body or soul), wouldn't you want to tell them? Acting upon a same-sex attraction is harmful to a person's soul because it is not what God intended for sex. It's not fulfilling because it can never be complete sexual union that has the capability of bringing about new life. And for these reasons, not judging a person's heart is not the same thing as saying you're okay with how they act sexually. Be careful to never assume someone is living in sin, just because you know they experience same-sex attractions. You have to have a very close, trusted relationship with someone in order to walk with them toward virtue.

If someone "comes out" to you, how should you react?

If one of your friends "comes out" to you, you should respond with charity and compassion. It is always difficult and takes a great deal of courage to be vulnerable with another person, so you need to realize that this person trusts you with this delicate information. If in coming out to you, they are afraid you will reject them and their friendship, this is a great time to reaffirm that you care about them and that nothing will change in your friendship.

Why is it important to talk to someone you trust if you're struggling with sin?

Your struggle with sin doesn't have to be an internal battle that you're fighting on your own. Note that in the case of experiencing same-sex attractions (or any type of attractions), it is not the experience of the attractions themselves that are the committed sin – rather it is what you do with them that determines if you are committing a sin! Either way, what helps greatly is to go to a strong, faithful older friend, youth minister, parent, or a priest and tell them about what you're dealing with. Chances are they'll find you to be so courageous and offer you great advice on how to combat what you're struggling with. Ask them to keep you accountable and ask them to pray for you. If you're serious about ending your struggle with sin, ask someone to walk with you on your journey to freedom. Even Christ didn't carry His cross on His own – Saint Simon of Cyrene helped Him!

CHAPTER 9

Can I be friends with people who aren't Catholic?

Of course! These friendships can bear goodness in many ways. However do recognize when certain friendships may be pulling you away from Christ. AJ recognized that he was idolizing his friends and using his friends to replace his relationship with Christ. If your friends aren't pushing you toward sainthood, pray for an increase in friendships where Christ is at the center.

Why didn't God take away AJ's temptations when he prayed that he wouldn't feel this way anymore?

God gives each of us the experiences and graces that we need to become the people that we are meant to be. We usually think of sufferings, trials and temptations as bad, but actually they're really important to our spiritual development. In other words, sometimes our problems seem to be getting in the way of the things that we would like to accomplish – but they're actually a means by which God reveals what He intends us to accomplish. Our weaknesses and temptations also help us to rely on God, rather than on our own strength: that's why when St. Paul prayed for God to remove the thorn in his side, God replied, "My grace is enough for you" (2 Corinthians 12:6-9).

If the love of Jesus is enough for us, why do we feel lonely?

God is not a solitary individual sitting up in heaven. He's a community of three persons: the Father, the Son and the Holy Spirit. When He made human beings in His "image and likeness" He made us to live in community, just like He does. One of the difficulties that people experiencing same-sex attractions confront in our society is that we often think of marriage as being the only way of living in a really intimate communion with other people. The Christian tradition, however, has always offered a variety of different forms of communal life that image and reflect different aspects of Divine Love. Examples would include: monasteries and convents, lay communities, parish life, deep friendship, or holy partnerships (like some of the saints who worked closely together to grow in virtue). Our experience of the love of Christ is always mediated by other people – most especially by our Mother Mary, who we call "mediatrix of grace" because it was through her co-operation with God that Christ came into the world. Loneliness reminds us that we are meant to receive God's love from other people, and to pour out His love to other people.

CHAPTER 10

Is it okay to be angry with God?

Yes, the God of the universe can handle your anger. He doesn't want you to bottle it up, He wants you to be your genuine self and to run to Him with your anger, confusion, and wrestle with His truth or plans. Don't forget that we are human and take everything we hear and learn and filter them through our subjective emotions and life experiences. God and His ways are much greater than we can possibly comprehend. That's why we need to rely on Christ and why He gives us His Church to help us.

However, it is not okay to give up on God. We can be angry and frustrated with Him, but we need to continue the relationship. If we give up on God, we close ourselves off to the grace, healing, and love that He pours out on us – even when we are angry. We have to remember that we can use those times of anger and frustration to rely on grace and grow in virtue if we choose to.

AJ talks about his straight friends having sex and how it's wrong just like having gay sex is wrong. If they're both wrong, why do some Catholics say that being gay is "disordered"? Isn't that offensive?

The word "disordered" has been used to describe homosexual actions in some documents of the Catholic Church. This word was never meant to be offensive or derogatory. It refers to the actions, but not the people. It means that an act is not ordered toward its proper end.

We are inherently good because we are all sons and daughters of God. Sin of any kind is disordered because it harms our relationship with God. Sin at the very core is bad. That means that actions like stealing, lying, murder, hatred, pride, sexual sins, gossip...etc. are all disordered because they disrupt God's plan for our lives which is a relationship with Him and heaven. In the same vein, homosexual acts are disordered because they are contradictory to God's plan for sex – that sex be free, total, faithful, and fruitful within the Sacrament of Marriage. Same-sex attractions can never be ordered toward the sexual union of spouses who are complementary in nature and whose union can lead to the procreation of new human beings. Homosexual acts are counter to how we were structurally created, so engaging in them is sort of a slap in the face to the one who created us – as though we are saying God's magnificent work of art (the human body) was wrong and we are going to use it how we like and not how He intended.

The important thing to remember is that all inclination to sin is disordered, and that people cannot be disordered. Sin does have a profound effect on us and our will – in fact, the more we sin, the more distorted our will can become through the effect of sin. This can lead to more sinning and get us stuck in a cycle that is dangerous and deadly. Each of us is precious and loved in the eyes of God – and God offers us mercy, especially through the Sacrament of Reconciliation, to help restore us when we sin.

Why can't AJ get married to a man if he loves him and wants to be committed to him?

AJ knows that a sexual relationship with a man is contrary to God's plan for sex and marriage. God created the Sacrament of Marriage the way it is (between one man and one woman) for a reason and it's not up to us to change what God has established, and which we know through Scripture and the Traditions of the Church. Because men and women were created different and unique, they each bring something totally different and unique to a marriage – and also something unique and different within the parent-child relationship, if there were to be children involved. These differences are complementary and help to make a marriage healthy and holy — both for the couple and for the children.

Speaking of children, they're an essential part of what marriage is all about. When a couple has sex inside of the Sacrament of Marriage, it serves two purposes: procreation and unity. (That's what naturally happens when a couple has sex, right?) When one of those two components is taken away it destroys the nature of sex. A destruction of the nature of sex, something we do with our bodies, harms us as people. We are made of a body and soul and you cannot separate the two; what you do with your body matters to your soul. If you willfully and purposefully take away the unitive nature of sex through an act of rape or sexual abuse — that violates the nature of sex, and violates the person.

If you willfully and purposefully take out the procreative aspect of sex by homosexual acts, contraception, or even "forms of straight sex" (you get the idea) it also violates the nature of sex and therefore violates the person. It goes against what God made sex for and what God made us for. That's why no matter what, the Catholic Church is never going to approve of gay marriage. As a faithful, practicing Catholic who loves God, AJ has learned to understand and accept this teaching, regardless of the fact that it is difficult and some days it may not be what he wants... it's still the eternal truth... and he wants that more than temporary physical or emotional satisfaction.

Why does AJ "have to" live alone? How will he be able to give and receive love?

AJ knows that in the future he may live alone because he has decided that for him, it's not a good idea to live with another guy that he may be attracted to, or with a guy who may have feelings for him. It's too tempting. He also believes that marriage is only between a man and a woman, so he doesn't want to get married to a man. AJ doesn't know for sure what the future holds but living alone doesn't have to mean that he will be lonely. There are lots of other ways to have a full life and stay connected to other people, aside from having a partner to live with. Each of us have a vocation to love God and other people which can be lived out in so many beautiful ways apart from a sexual relationship.

Many people who don't end up marrying—for whatever reason—find other ways to lead lives full of love. Some people share their lives and their homes with their closest friends. They may live in "intentional communities," homes where many Christians live together in order to love God and serve those in need. Or they may be deeply connected to their parish community. When a parish community is able to provide a sense of family for its members, people experience the joy of being nourished, supported, and fulfilled. These people are much more likely to remain committed to striving after lives of virtue (like that of celibacy) if they are already living in accord with Church teaching, while those who are in dissent are much more likely to come to see celibacy as a viable option if they're enmeshed in a vibrant community that provides for their spiritual and emotional needs.

Some people are able to be spiritual mothers and fathers to others who have been isolated or marginalized - at places such as crisis pregnancy centers, homeless outreach, elder care, prison ministry, or care for the disabled. Self-giving is a really important part of human fulfillment, and when people lack a means of providing self-giving love to others, it tends to make them unhappy.

Others live very full lives by sharing themselves with the world creatively through artistic and intellectual pursuits. Having a creative outlet and creating something of value to be left behind is a way to love others. We often think of love wholly in terms of relationship, but it also has a creative/expressive dimension - God was loving the world into being for billions and billions of years before any people came into existence for Him to have a relationship with.

If you're afraid that your future will be lonely and loveless, it might be useful to seek out mentors who aren't married. Find people who are leading lives you admire — maybe teachers, godparents, those who serve others in your community — and ask yourself what you can learn from them about leading a fruitful life outside of marriage. Remember that marriage is not the right vocation for everyone!

Right now there aren't very many role models for Christians who experience same-sex attraction. That means that you may find yourself building a life that doesn't look much like your parents' lives, or your siblings' lives. It's especially important for people in more unusual life paths to seek out guidance from more experienced mentors, like priests or well-formed laypeople.

Trust that God will help you to give and receive love. You may live by yourself, as AJ plans to; you may live with friends or in community; but no matter what, you will not need to face your struggles and celebrate your victories alone.